"I have sung hymns and worship songs for decades and have repeated the lyrics hundreds of times. Truth be told, I don't always have a full grasp of their meaning. *The Words We Sing* is an extremely well-written, informative, and enjoyable look into many of these terms, with definitions, composers' insights, and stories around these timeless songs. I only wish I would have had this wonderful reference much sooner."

—GREG NELSON
Composer, Arranger, and Producer
Grammy and Dove Awards Winner

"I hold my calling as a worshiper of the Most High God in high regard. There is nothing I do on earth or will do in heaven that is more important than offering myself to Him in a life of worship. And I never want to be flippant about the songs I write or sing or lead when I am singing to God in worship. That is why I love this book. Nan brings us great wisdom and insight, and as we better understand the songs we sing in worship, our intimacy with the Lord grows, and our worship experience deepens. And those very experiences are part of what lead us to living transformed lives."

—TRAVIS COTTRELL
Composer, Worship Leader, Recording Artist

"I expected a reference book but found so much more. *The Words We Sing* brings an even greater appreciation to the songs I have loved for a lifetime."

—DAVE CLARK
Songwriter and Author

THE *WORDS* WE *SING*

THE  WORDS WE SING

NAN CORBITT ALLEN

BEACON HILL PRESS
OF KANSAS CITY

ISBN 978-0-8341-2550-6

Printed in the
United States of America

Book Design: Arthur Cherry

All Scripture quotations not otherwise designated are from the
Holy Bible, New International Version® (NIV®). Copyright © 1973,
1978, 1984 by International Bible Society. Used by permission
of Zondervan Publishing House. All rights reserved.

Permission to quote from the following additional copyrighted
version of the Bible is acknowledged with appreciation:
The New American Standard Bible® (NASB®), © copyright The
Lockman Foundation 1960, 1962, 1963, 1968, 1971, 1972,
1973, 1975, 1977, 1995.

Scripture quotations marked KJV are from the King James
Version.

Library of Congress Cataloging-in-Publication Data

  Allen, Nan Corbitt.
  The words we sing : bringing meaning to worship / Nan Corbitt Allen.
     p. cm.
  Includes bibliographical references (p.   ).
  ISBN 978-0-8341-2550-6 (hardcover)
  1. Hymns—History and criticism. I. Title.
  BV310.A44 2010
  264'.23—dc22

                                      2010027178

10 9 8 7 6 5 4 3 2 1

CONTENTS

INTRODUCTION

Christian music is an official genre of music. I'm sure that fact comes as no surprise.

From music industry publications to radio charts to iTunes, it's in a class by itself. It comes in various styles: traditional, hip-hop, country, bluegrass, rock, pop—you name it. However, it's the only genre of music completely defined by lyrics. So shouldn't we all be more careful of the lyrics we write, lead others in singing, and embrace as truth?

That's the purpose of this book—to unwrap these words and phrases in Christian song lyrics that touch our hearts and satisfy our minds.

 ABBA

There's a lot of great drama at the airport. I like to go there just to watch the people who are waiting and the ones who are arriving to see if I can read their stories.

One recent Christmastime we were waiting at the airport for some very dear family members to arrive. As we waited, I watched a family, a mother and three children, waiting too. The oldest was a boy who looked to be about ten or so, then another boy, maybe seven or eight, and a little blonde-haired girl still in diapers and sucking on a pacifier. Great anticipation was obvious on all their faces.

A small swell of people immerged from the gate, and then another. At the beginning of the third surge, the one they were waiting for arrived at last. He was dressed in military fatigues and was shouldering a duffle bag. From the looks of things, he had been overseas for a long time.

As soon as he cleared the security checkpoint, he dropped his duffle bag, knelt down, and opened his arms. The three happy children ran into them. Daddy had come home.

The same name those children called their father, *Daddy,* is the English version of the word *Abba.*

Abba receives its first introduction to the Bible from Jesus himself. In Aramaic, the Hebrew dialect that Jesus spoke, the word indicated an intimate relationship between father and child. Some commentaries stress that slaves were forbidden to address the head of the family by this title. It was reserved only for natural-born or adopted children.

As Jesus was praying in the Garden of Gethsemane right before His crucifixion, He was heard calling to God, "Abba."

> "Abba, Father," he said, "everything is possible for you. Take this cup from me. Yet not what I will, but what you will" *(Mark 14:36).*

> Paul picks up on this reference to God as coined by His only natural-born Son.

Those who are led by the Spirit of God are sons of God. For you did not receive a spirit that makes you a slave again to fear, but you received the Spirit of sonship. And by him we cry, "Abba, Father." The Spirit himself testifies with our spirit that we are God's children *(Romans 8:14-16)*.

Because you are sons, God sent the Spirit of his Son into our hearts, the Spirit who calls out, "Abba, Father" *(Galatians 4:6)*.

Because we are God's children, through adoption after our salvation, we have the right to call our Heavenly Father, the Creator of the universe, *Abba*.

Steve Fry[1] captures the beauty of the phrase is his song entitled "Abba Father"[2]

> *Abba Father, Abba Father*
> *Deep within my soul I cry.*
> *Abba Father, Abba Father,*
> *I will never cease to love You.*

Fry writes,

> I had the privilege of being a youth pastor for over nine years. As a matter of fact, I started rather young—17, to be exact. Working with my peers was especially rewarding during those days, because the Jesus movement had a full head of steam. Soon, hundreds of young people were in our youth group.

Culture then—as now—was rapidly changing. The majority of teenagers in our youth group came from difficult family backgrounds. They were looking for ways to understand God that would help them connect to Him.

In a pursuit of understanding God better, we began to explore what the idea of His role Father meant. In particular, we looked at that passage in Romans 8 that says that we have received the spirit of sonship whereby we can cry, "Abba Father." In studying this, I was struck by the fact that to say "Abba Father" in our day would be to say something like "Papa God."

This revelation, at least to me, did not suggest casual flippancy or an inappropriate chumminess with the Lord; rather, it suggested a depth of intimacy that I had not known before.

It was during this season in which Abba Father was making himself real to me that I decided to go alone into our church sanctuary very late at night to worship. I sat down at the big Baldwin grand piano—I think it must've been close to midnight—and began to pour out my adoration before the Lord in spontaneous worship. This little chorus was birthed within five minutes as I sat there worshiping God. It perhaps was one of the quickest downloads from heaven I ever received as a songwriter! It captured in a moment the heart of a young man still in his teens whose chief aim in life was to know God.

The song "Abba Father" is about capturing the full-faced innocence that we as God's children can have with Him. It is as if He is giving us permission to come as His little ones, crawl upon His lap, and embrace Him with the tender words "Papa God." Such an approach is not disrespectful or inappropriately familiar. It is a term that suggests a depth of intimacy and trust that we as believers can know and have with God.[3]

ADONAI / LORD

We once took our children to a medieval dinner, where we saw riders on horseback reenact a medieval jousting tournament as we cheered and ate with our fingers. That night I wondered what it would have been like to live in medieval times. Since I probably wouldn't have been born into nobility, I would have lived among the serf class and no doubt been subjected to a lord. In that case I might have had a better understanding of what the word *Adonai* means. Since the concept is foreign these days, I've had to search for the meaning.

The word *adonai* was the Old Testament Hebrew word for "lord," and it referred to God but was sometimes used for one human's rule over another. Its literal translation is "One who has power and exercises it responsibly; someone or something having power, authority, or influence."

For a long time God was referred to as Jehovah, the Self-Existent One. At some point, however, the Jews felt it improper to speak the name "Jehovah" or "Yahweh" (see Jehovah/Yahweh), so they often substituted *Adonai*. It first appears in a conversation that Abram had with God, and it's recorded in Genesis 15.

In many Bible translations the word Lord is frequently written in all capital letters to signify that it refers to "Yahweh." But when the word is written with only the letter "l" capitalized, then it means "Adonai."

> He [God] said to him, "I am the Lord [Yahweh] who brought you out of Ur of the Chaldeans, to give you this land to possess it."

> He said, "O Lord [Adonai] God, how may I know that I will possess it?" *(Genesis 15:7-8, NASB)*.

In the New Testament world the Greek word *kurios* meant "lord," but, again, it did not always refer to God. It was a title of respect to an official or to a father or head of the household. Jesus was referred to as "lord" in that way, but only as other respectable people were. Jesus was more often referred to as *Rabbi,* which meant "Teacher." It was not until after Jesus' resurrection that He was called "Lord" in a way that made Him equal to God. Thomas, after seeing and touching the resurrected Jesus, proclaims Him "My Lord and my God!" *(John 20:28)*.

In the song "Praise Adonai," by Paul Baloche, the Hebrew word for Lord is used in an expression of praise to Him.

> *Praise Adonai!*
> *From the rising of the sun*
> *'Til the end of every day.*
> *Praise Adonai!*
> *All the nations of the earth,*
> *All the angels and the saints,*
> *Sing praise.*[1]

Baloche writes, "We were in Israel and we listened to the Hebrew prayers being prayed at the Wailing Wall. And I could hear the word 'Adonai' a lot. And that just got me thinking about the name and how that is the name that David used to call upon the Lord. It is just a beautiful expression."[2]

ALLELUIAH / HALLELUJAH

You might hear the word *hallelujah* spoken today when something good happens. But *alleluia* isn't heard in everyday speech as much, even though we sing it in worship songs and hymns, especially in Christmas carols.

The two common spellings of the same word are due to the way the Hebrews spelled it (English equivalent *hallelujah* and the Greek version *alleluia*). They mean the same thing, however: God be praised!

The word came out of another Hebrew word, *hallel,* which literally means "a song of praise." The Levites (the priestly tribe of ancient Israel) were given the special assignment of singing these praise songs. The "Hallel" is now a Jewish prayer that's a verbatim recitation of Psalms 113—118. Today it's used in Jewish praise and thanksgiving celebrations and holidays.

A beautiful chorus "Antiphonal Praise," written and sung by Steve Green,[1] is a pure praise song to God.

> We worship You, Almighty God;
> In You alone is our delight.
> We worship You, oh holy God,
> And lift our voice to sing Your praise.
> Alleluia! Alleluia! Alleluia! Alleluia![2]

Green writes,

In the early years of singing I searched for ways to help the audience express praise to God. One morning I began humming a melody and then added simple lyrics. When the heart is full of adoration, sometimes the only expression that suffices is "Alleluia." That night we used the song in our gathering, and I was thrilled to hear a whole congregation lift their voices in unison and sing with all their hearts, "Alleluia."[3]

ALPHA AND OMEGA

I love parades. Because I love them, I remember what a wise person once said about them. He said that life is like a parade— "Too bad that we only get to see what's directly in front of us and not the whole thing at once." (This was a reference to our finite and therefore narrow view of life.)

From eighth grade through high school, I was in the marching band. Every Friday afternoon before a home game, the band and cheerleaders lined up and marched down the main street of my hometown. But I realized once that I hadn't seen very many parades except those I was in. And in the position of participant, I got an even more limited perspective on the event than a normal observer.

What must it be like to see something like a parade—a big one like Macy's Thanksgiving Day Parade—from a "whole" perspective? Beginning, end, middle—all at once.

That's the idea behind the phrase *Alpha and Omega.* These words are simply the first and last letters of the Greek alphabet, and the phrase was used in reference to God, but only in the New Testament. However, before Greek became the language of the written Word, Isaiah put the idea into place.

> This is what the Lord says—Israel's King and Redeemer, the Lord Almighty: I am the first and I am the last; apart from me there is no God *(Isaiah 44:6)*.

Then we skip to Revelation, where John writes the exact phrase as words of God, who claims,

> "I am the Alpha and the Omega . . . who is, and who was, and who is to come, the Almighty *(Revelation 1:8)*.

This phrase expresses the Almighty's eternal existence (before time and forevermore) and His control over all things (all history and to all things future). He sees His whole creation from the first whistle blown of the drum majorette to the last trumpet sound in the back of the line—beginning, end, all in between.

One of my favorite older hymns is "Love Divine, All Loves Excelling." The second verse says,

Breathe, O breathe Thy loving Spirit
Into every troubled breast!
Let us all in Thee inherit;
Let us find that promised rest.
Take away our bent to sinning;
Alpha and Omega be;
End of faith, as its Beginning,
Set our hearts at liberty.[1]

This hymn text speaks of God's being the Alpha and Omega as a freeing fact. Because He knows all, sees all, and is over all, we can find "that promised rest."

AMEN

The "amen corner" of the church I grew up in wasn't really a corner. It was a group of people who were, let's just say, more vocal than others during our worship services. When the preacher said something they agreed with, they often punctuated it with a hearty "Amen!" or "Hallelujah!"

Nowadays the word *amen* almost always ends a prayer, and it can be spoken, or in some churches it's sung. Believe it or not, because of this many churchgoers believe that it means "the end." But the word means so much more. It's from a Hebrew word meaning "a proclamation that is certain, sure and credible, truthful and faithful. Often translated as 'so be it.'"

In Old Testament times it was used to show acceptance of a message, an oath, or another spoken proclamation. In Deuteronomy 27 Moses rehearses the Israelites on what would happen once they had crossed over the Jordan River (See JORDAN) into the Promised Land. He tells them how the land will be divided among the tribes and what the Levites (the priests) will say to them at that time. There were twelve curses that the priests would use to warn the people of misdeeds, and after each one the people were to respond with an "amen." For example:

"Cursed is the man who carves an image or casts an idol—a thing detestable to the LORD, the work of the craftsman's hands—and sets it up in secret." Then all the people shall say, "Amen!" "Cursed is the man who dishonors his father or his mother." Then all the people shall say, "Amen!" (Deuteronomy 27:15-16).

These were oaths that the people would speak, and in this context the word meant more than just the punctuation at the end of a prayer. It was a sort of binding agreement to the laws already sent down from Jehovah through Moses.

Jeremiah uses the word as a covenant with God. It's recorded in the eleventh chapter of the prophet's writings.

This is the word that came to Jeremiah from the LORD: "Listen to the terms of this covenant and tell them to the people of Judah and to those who live in Jerusalem. Tell them that this is what the Lord, the God of Israel, says: 'Cursed is the man who does not obey the terms of this covenant the terms I commanded your forefathers when I brought them out of Egypt, out of the iron-smelting furnace.' I said, 'Obey me and do everything I command you, and you will be my people, and I will be your God. Then I will fulfill the oath I swore to your forefathers, to give them a land flowing with milk and honey'—the land you possess today. I answered, 'Amen, Lord'" *(Jeremiah 11:1-5).*

Jesus used *amen* to emphasize and affirm the truth of His own statements. However, English translations use *verily, truly,* or *I tell you the truth* for the same word as *amen.* Jesus never said these affirmations at the end of a statement but always at the beginning. In Matthew 5 He said,

> Verily I say unto you, Till heaven and earth pass, one jot or one tittle shall in no wise pass from the law, till all be fulfilled *(Matthew 5:18, KJV).*

In Revelation 3:14 John calls Jesus "the Amen"—

> To the angel of the church in Laodicea write: These are the words of the Amen, the faithful and true witness, the ruler of God's creation.

Some believe that this was an indication that Jesus' words were credible and faithful. Others add that John might have meant that Jesus would have the "last word."

Matt Redman, Josiah Bell, and Robert Marvin wrote the song "Yes and Amen," which is sung as an acceptance of God's will and guidance.

Matt Redman adds, "I'd wanted to write around this theme for a long time. A song with a heart cry that says, 'Anything you ask of me I want to say yes, and anything you have planned for my life I want to be in agreement, saying Amen.'"[1]

The last verse of the hymn "Praise to the Lord, the Almighty" uses the affirming word. This verse seems to be an invitation to join in praise to God.

> *Praise to the Lord,*
> *O let all that is in me adore Him!*
> *All that hath life and breath,*
> *Come now with praises before Him.*
> *Let the Amen*
> *Sound from His people again;*
> *Gladly for aye we adore Him!*[2]

By the way, the word *aye,* which could be synonymous with *amen,* as in an affirmative vote, probably meant "always" or "forever" instead.

ANCIENT OF DAYS

The prophet Daniel used the phrase *Ancient of Days,* which literally means one advanced in days, as a name for God. Daniel indicating that God was preexistent, beyond time. The phrase also refers to one who forwards time or rules over it. Daniel was the only biblical writer who referred to God in this way. In Daniel 7 he writes about a dream he had. It is in this description—and in no other place—that Daniel refers to his vision of God as "The Ancient of Days."

As I looked, thrones were set in place, and the Ancient of Days took his seat *(Daniel 7:9).*

Daniel then describes God even further:

His clothing was as white as snow; the hair of his head was white like wool. His throne was flaming with fire, and its wheels were all ablaze *(Daniel 7:9).*

In this vision "the Ancient of Days" seemed to be like a judge presiding over a court.

> In my vision at night I looked, and there before me was one like a son of man, coming with the clouds of heaven. He approached the Ancient of Days and was led into his presence. He was given authority, glory and sovereign power; all peoples, nations and men of every language worshiped him. His dominion is an everlasting dominion that will not pass away, and his kingdom is one that will never be destroyed *(Daniel 7:13-14)*.

The "son of man" apparently was presented before the judge, and the judge gave Him everlasting rule of all that exists. Most scholars believe this is a prophecy declaring that Jesus (the Son of Man) ruled equally with God.

Some sources believe that Daniel's name for God was a reference to His being eternal, wise, and sovereign. (See REIGN/SOVEREIGN.)

The majestic hymn "O Worship the King" is the first song that comes to mind that uses this phrase.

> *O worship the King, all glorious above,*
> *And gratefully sing His wonderful love;*
> *Our Shield and Defender, the Ancient of Days,*
> *Pavilioned in splendor, and girded with praise.*[1]

Travis Cottrell and Chance Scoggins[2] wrote the song "Now and Forevermore," which uses "Ancient of Days" in the chorus synonymously with "God of our Fathers."

> *Holy Lord, receive our praise,*
> *God of our Fathers, the Ancient of Days.*
> *You are worthy, worthy now and forevermore.*[3]

Chance writes,

When I wrote this lyric, I had been struck by Daniel's comparisons of God's eternal power and dominion in contrast to man's frailty, even at our best. Even the greatest of kings would fall. When I read his description of the Ancient of Days, I thought, *Wow! He's still that same God, the Ancient.* Generations before me and after me will pass, but He will always endure. And in those pages I understood a part of God I had certainly heard about—but this time I knew it for myself. Even in this moment, that is a mind-boggling thought. The God of our fathers will be the God of our great, great, great grandchildren. He has been—and will always be just as worthy, just as present, just as loving, as gracious, just as mighty to save, as mighty in battle—just as "God" as He is today, and as He was in those ancient pages. Long after our names and legacies are forgotten, He Is. Each generation joins to sing Jesus is Lord, Now and Forevermore.[4]

 ATONEMENT

Everybody has heard stories of husbands who send flowers or gifts to apologize.

With my own heartfelt apology if I'm making something divine too colloquial, it seems that this illustration might help to define the word *atonement.* It is "a gift or offering that reconciles or mends a broken relationship."

Though the concept was around as far back as Cain and Abel, the word *atonement* didn't come into scriptural writings until Moses's time. While the Israelites were wandering in the wilderness, God started setting a standard of reconciliation with Him through animal sacrifice (see BLOOD). First, the Israelites were to build a tabernacle (see TABERNACLE), then equip it with altars so that the priests could officially accept the sacrifices of the people. In Exodus instructions were given for the proper way to make atonement or to be reconciled to God.

> Sacrifice a bull each day as a sin offering to make atonement. Purify the altar by making atonement for it, and anoint it to consecrate it. For seven days make atonement for the altar and consecrate it. Then the altar will be most holy, and whatever touches it will be holy *(Exodus 29:36-37)*.

Not only were the people to be reconciled, but the altars had to be atoned for—or made holy—as well (see HOLY).

Some writers have broken the word *atonement* into its parts in hopes that its meaning will be made clear. AT-ONE-MENT is this play on the word. Again, this may be an oversimplification of a deep theological concept, but it may help us remember what it means and how it has been used.

There's the atonement or gift of reconciliation, but why is there a need to be reconciled to God anyway? Isaiah said it this way:

> Your iniquities have separated you from your God; your sins have hidden his face from you, so that he will not hear *(Isaiah 59:2)*.

Apparently, our sins have broken our relationship to God, and the blood of animals was once able to open the door to reconciliation. It followed the tradition, then, of blood sacrifice when Jesus allowed His to atone for our sins.

If, when we were God's enemies, we were reconciled to him through the death of his Son, how much more, having been reconciled, shall we be saved through his life! Not only is this so, but we also rejoice in God through our Lord Jesus Christ, through whom we have now received reconciliation *(Romans 5:10-11).*

True atonement happens when the offending party is indeed penitent and the offended party is willing to forgive. Amends were made for our offenses to God once and for all with the sacrifice Christ made of himself. The book of Hebrews is rich with truth about atonement. Here's just one statement:

How much more, then, will the blood of Christ, who through the eternal Spirit offered himself unblemished to God, cleanse our consciences from acts that lead to death, so that we may serve the living God! *(Hebrews 9:14).*

Though many songs allude to the reconciliation of God and humanity, Fanny Crosby just came right out and used *atonement* in the opening lines of her famous hymn "To God Be the Glory"

To God be the glory, great things He hath done;
So loved He the world that He gave us His Son,
Who yielded His life an atonement for sin,
And opened the life-gate that all may go in.[1]

Though it's not clear what a "life-gate" is, it's clear that our reconciliation to God was the yielded life of God's Son.

BALM IN GILEAD

Jeremiah, the weeping prophet, threw the term *balm in Gilead* out there in one of his many laments.

Since my people are crushed, I am crushed; I mourn, and horror grips me. Is there no balm in Gilead? Is there no physician there? Why then is there no healing for the wound of my people? *(Jeremiah 8:21-22)*.

Gilead, which was east of the Jordan River (see JORDAN), northeast of the Dead Sea, was rugged country. It had peaks that reached over 3,500 feet and grassy plains that were good for flocks and herds of all kinds. It was during the times of the later patriarchs, the judges, and the kings of Israel that Gilead was considered a city of refuge.

Its greatest claim to fame, however, was the production of a resin from the balsam tree that was made into a fragrant salve thought to have powerful healing properties. Not only was the balm used for healing, but it also had use as a cosmetic substance.

Why Jeremiah chose to use this metaphor in his lament is unclear, but the great Negro spiritual apparently was itself a healing balm to early American slaves.

> *There is a balm in Gilead*
> *To make the wounded whole.*
> *There is a balm in Gilead,*
> *To heal the sin-sick soul.*
> *Sometimes I feel discouraged*
> *And think my work's in vain,*
> *But then the Holy Spirit*
> *Revives my soul again.*[1]

 BANNER

Banner is a word that's seen a transformation with the use of the Internet. Who hasn't gone to a site and seen advertisements for other products and services scrolling or pulsing in his or her peripheral vision? Most of the time these ads are actually links to sponsors. Those are called "banner ads."

In the biblical sense, a banner wasn't really so different from the cyber-use of the word. Mostly used in battle, they were markers, indicators, signals, and rallying points for soldiers or entire tribes. In a sense they advertised or proclaimed the identification of the group gathered under it.

Banner was also a name attributed to God. Here's the story from Exodus 17:

Moses said to Joshua, "Choose some of our men and go out to fight the Amalekites. Tomorrow I will stand on top of the hill with the staff of God in my hands." So Joshua fought the Amalekites as Moses had ordered, and Moses, Aaron and Hur went to the top of the hill. As long as Moses held up his hands, the Israelites were winning, but whenever he lowered his hands, the Amalekites were winning. When Moses' hands grew tired, the people took a stone and put it under him and he sat on it. Aaron and Hur held Moses' hands up—one on one side, one on the other—so that his hands remained steady until sunset. So Joshua overcame the Amalekite army with the sword.

Then the LORD said to Moses, "Write this on a scroll as something to be remembered and make sure that Joshua hears it, because I will completely blot out the memory of Amalek from under heaven."

Moses built an altar and called it The LORD is my Banner. He said, "For hands were lifted up to the throne of the LORD. The LORD will be at war against the Amalekites from generation to generation" *(Exodus 17:9-16)*.

Jehovah-nissi (see JEHOVAH) was the Hebrew term that means Moses proclaimed God to be his banner—his marker, the One with which he identifies.

In earlier hymns, the banner represented a signal to engage in warfare, perhaps spiritual warfare, against Satan. One that comes to mind is "The Banner of the Cross."[1]

> *There's a royal banner*
> *Given for display*
> *To the soldiers of the King;*
> *As an ensign fair*
> *We lift it up today,*
> *While as ransomed ones we sing.*
>
> *Marching on, marching on,*
> *For Christ count everything but loss!*
> *And to crown Him King, toil and sing*
> *'Neath the banner of the cross*[1]

Modern song lyrics that speak of the banner often are asking believers to raise the Banner. "Not to Us," written by Chris Tomlin and Jesse Reeves, does just that.

> *The cross before me, the world behind;*
> *No turning back, raise the banner high.*
> *It's not for me, it's all for You.*[2]

This is a song we sing unto God with a declaration that we will proclaim, promote, advocate—advertise—Him to the world. In the contemporary use of the word *banner,* this is a call to lift up the cause of Christ wherever we go.

BLESS / BLESSED

"Bless your heart!" was once an expression of sympathy—a least in the South. It's taken on a little more of a sardonic tone these days, however, and its attitude has become one of condescension and pity. But this modern usage does not come close to describing the words *bless* or *blessed* or *blessing* as they were used in the Bible and therefore what we intend them to mean in our songs.

There were many meanings of the word in Scripture and various ways to gain or grant blessing.

God Blessed Humanity

God created man in his own image, in the image of God he created him; male and female he created them.

God blessed them and said to them, "Be fruitful and increase in number; fill the earth and subdue it. Rule over the fish of the sea and the birds of the air and over every living creature that moves on the ground" *(Genesis 1:27-28).*

In this case the word *blessed* means to grant happiness, prosperity, and even fertility. But it also implies that humanity was "set apart" (see HOLY, HOLINESS) because of God's favor upon humanity.

In a little-known story of the Hebrews' attempt at acquiring the Promised Land during Moses' time, Balak, the Moabite king, asked his soothsayer, Balaam, to curse the Israelites, to ensure Moab's conquest over them. However, the soothsayer found he could speak only God's words of blessing to the Israelites instead of a curse.

Balaam told the king, recorded in Numbers 23:20,

I have received a command to bless; he has blessed, and I cannot change it.

God's blessing was hard to reverse once it was pronounced.

The old hymn "Count Your Blessings" encourages us to be amazed at all that God has done for us. The chorus says,

Count your blessings, name them one by one;
Count your blessings, see what God hath done;
Count your blessings, name them one by one;
Count your many blessings, see what God hath done.[1]

A Person Blessed God

The psalmist writes,

> Bless the LORD, O my soul: and all that is within me, bless his holy name *(Psalm 103:1, KJV)*.

Here the word means to praise or to make known God's existence and power. This definition is more prominent in today's songwriting, but its background goes back to another great songwriter of another day.

David used the word as he praised the Lord in a prayer found in 1 Chronicles:

> David blessed the LORD before all the congregation: and David said, "Blessed be thou, LORD God of Israel our father, for ever and ever" *(1 Chronicles 29:10, KJV)*.

David then invited the congregation to do the same thing:

> "Now bless the LORD your God." And all the congregation blessed the LORD God of their fathers, and bowed down their heads, and worshipped the LORD, and the king *(1 Chronicles 29:20, KJV)*.

Not to be confused with the blessing of God to humanity, which brings with it immutable power, this reference to humanity blessing God is merely an act of praise.

Most of the songs we sing today that use the word *bless* or *blessed* are intended as a praise phrase, as in Don Moen's "Blessed Be the Name of the Lord"

> Blessed be the name of the Lord,
> He is worthy to be praised and adored;
> So we lift up holy hands in one accord,
> Singing, Blessed be the name, blessed be the name,
> Blessed be the name of the Lord![2]

This song is an outpouring of corporate praise. Don Moen[3] writes,

I don't have any great revelation on the word *blessed,* but primarily it was birthed out of Psalm 34. David said, "I will bless the Lord at all times, His praise shall continually be in my mouth."

To bless (to praise God) is really a decision we make. It is an act of our will. We choose to bless the Lord, no matter what the circumstance. When things are going well in our lives, it is much easier to bless the Lord and give Him praise. It's quite another thing when life has thrown you a curve ball, and you feel unprepared or unready to respond with praise and blessing. It is much easier to ask the question, "why?"

When David wrote Psalm 34, I believe it was during a time when he was hiding from Saul, who was trying to kill him. David asked many questions of God during that time but ultimately responded with, "I will bless the Lord at all times," including those times that were hurtful and didn't make sense. David didn't deny that he was afraid, but he realized the importance of offering praise and blessing to God during those times.

This chorus, "Blessed Be the Name of the Lord," is a very simple chorus that came to me as I was being introduced to sing one Sunday morning in Texas. I intended to sing another song, but I couldn't move ahead until I had shared with the audience this simple chorus. I have heard the criticism—some justified—about simple praise and worship songs that have no substance to them. However, this simple song is filled with solid truth.

Blessed be the name of the Lord. We choose to bless Him. He is worthy to be praised and adored, no matter what the circumstance. He is worthy!

So we lift up holy hands in one accord. We are instructed to lift holy hands in 1 Timothy 2:8.

The only thing left to do is to "Bless His Holy Name."[4]

Steve Green recently recorded a Babbie Mason/Kirk Kirkland song entitled "I Will Bless the Lord," which is drawn from an Old Testament song of praise, Psalm 103.

> *Bless the Lord,*
> *O my soul,*
> *And all that is within me*
> *Bless His name.*

Bless the Lord, O my soul
And all that is within me
Bless His name.
I will remember what He's done,
Counting my blessings, each and every one.
I am forgiven through His blood
And now I'm gonna sing.
Let all that is within me bless His name.[5]

Kirk writes,

Bless the LORD, O my soul, and all that is within me bless His holy name. *(Psalm 103:1)*

I've grown up singing several songs based on this scripture text and in recent years have been asking the question of what it means to bless the Lord. When I use the word *blessing,* I'm usually speaking of what the Lord has done for me; the many ways God has shown me favor or material things or opportunities. But I became intrigued with the idea that we could bless God. It was this scripture that led me to wonder.

The Hebrew word for *bless* means to kneel or adore. Webster says "to bless is to ask divine favor for, to praise, or to make happy."

So is this possible? Can I "make happy" the heart of God?

It's easy for me to think of God as difficult to please. After all, He is the Almighty Creator of the universe, completely holy and transcendent. I'm just little me, trying to live right, messing up rather often. If I were God, I think I'd be more disappointed in me than pleased. But what a beautiful thought, that this same God I've just described is pleased with me because of the blood of Christ on my life and that He can be moved like a perfect proud parent when He sees me doing my best to worship and serve Him. Oh, to live for the smile of heaven!

So I can bless the Lord with my praise and with my life! In that case, let all that is within me bless His holy name! The psalmist is holding nothing back. He wants to live and praise in such a way that makes happy the heart of God. And so do I![6]

This definition also applies when the word is used as an adjective, as in "Blessed Assurance," "Blessed Redeemer," or "Blessed Savior, We Adore Thee."

Where we got the pronunciation "bless-ed," making it a two-syllable word, is unclear. It is, however, poetic and therefore may be used because it's easier to sing.

There are three more definitions or usages of *bless* or *blessed* to explore. These aren't used as much in lyrics, but here, still, are their contexts.

A Person Blessed a Person

The story of the twin sons of Isaac, Jacob and Esau, is an account given to us in Genesis 27 of a tradition in which a father gave a blessing to an offspring. To be blessed, in this case, was to be granted authority and responsibility.

Humanity Blessed a Thing or Place

Blessed can be a word of dedication placed upon something or someone as an act of worship as if to separate it for God's use. (See HOLY, HOLINESS)

A pastor blesses the congregation before they leave a worship service, turning them out into the world to do God's work.

We bless the food at a meal. This is mostly a thanks offering but also, as has been recited around many a dinner table, the consecration of the food as nourishment to our bodies and our bodies to God's continued service.

An Attitude Granted by God

The word *blessed* appears in the New Testament, too, especially in the Beatitudes of the Sermon on the Mount (see Matthew 5:3-11). But the Greek word we translate as *blessed* is *makarios*, which means fortunate or happy. Its meaning changes just a bit from Hebrew or Greek and then to English. This meaning of the word isn't used often in songwriting either.

BLOOD

Are you washed in the blood of the Lamb?

This isn't a question you're likely to hear at the dinner table, but the mention of blood as a cleansing agent is pretty prominent in song lyrics of old as well as in recent writings. "O the Blood of Jesus" is from an anonymous source.

> *O the blood of Jesus,*
> *O the blood of Jesus,*
> *O the blood of Jesus,*
> *It washes white as snow.*[1]

Many songs report that there is power in the blood of Christ, as is stated in the song "There Is Power in the Blood"

Would you be free from the burden of sin?
There's power in the blood, power in the blood,
Would you o'er evil a victory win?
There's wonderful power in the blood.[2]

Andrea Crouch declares that "The Blood Will Never Lose Its Power" in his song written in the mid-1960s.

So where did the notion come from that the blood of Jesus has power and the ability to make us clean before God?

We have to go back to Exodus to find out.

Remember when the Israelites were trying to escape slavery in Egypt and God—through Moses—caused several plagues to be put upon the Egyptians to persuade Pharaoh to let the Jews go? The final plague, the death angel, was to bring death to the homes where blood was not applied to the entrance of the house.

> The blood will be a sign for you on the houses where you are; and when I see the blood, I will pass over you. No destructive plague will touch you when I strike Egypt *(Exodus 12:13)*.

The blood was to be taken from a lamb that had been slaughtered. This was significant because lambs—well, meat from any kind of animal—was scarce (see LAMB OF GOD), and the killing of a food-producing animal meant real sacrifice. But that's what God required of His people—then and now: obedience, sacrifice, trust without full understanding.

Not long after that, God put the blood sacrificial system in place. God's covenant was to be sealed by blood.

> When Moses went and told the people all the LORD's words and laws, they responded with one voice, "Everything the LORD has said we will do." Moses then wrote down everything the LORD had said. He got up early the next morning and built an altar at the foot of the mountain and set up twelve stone pillars representing the twelve tribes of Israel. Then he sent young Israelite men, and they offered burnt offerings and sacrificed young bulls as fellowship offerings to the LORD. Moses took half of the blood and put it in bowls, and the other half he sprinkled on the altar. Then he took the Book of the Covenant and read it to the people. They responded, "We will do everything the LORD has said; we will obey" *(Exodus 24:3-7).*

The importance of blood sacrifice was written into the Levitical writings and was declared to have atoning properties (see ATONEMENT). God says—

> The life of a creature is in the blood, and I have given it to you to make atonement for yourselves on the altar; it is the blood that makes atonement for one's life *(Leviticus 17:11).*

So blood is essential to life. Medical science has confirmed this. There is no substitute for blood. Nothing man-made can be used in its stead. That's why there are blood drives and donor programs, so the life-giving properties of blood can be passed from one life to another.

The Old Testament priests and prophets knew the importance of blood. Their worship required the spilling of animal blood and the use of it to consecrate—to make holy (see HOLY)—the altar and the people gathered around it.

But what does this have to do with Jesus' blood and its ability to repair our relationship with God?

The practice of animal sacrifice and the use of blood as a reparation of the relationship between God and humanity should have ended as soon as the priests entered the Temple in Jerusalem after the death of Jesus. They did discover that the veil of the Temple, which divided the holy of holies from the rest of the Temple, had been torn—from top to bottom—at the exact time Jesus breathed His last.

However, the practice continued for another generation, perhaps because the people could not understand how the blood of the prophet from Nazareth could have the same effect on their sins as the blood of sacrificed animals. The ritual of blood sacrifices continued until 70 A.D., when the Romans took over Jerusalem and destroyed the Temple.

The analogy of being washed in blood to make us clean is what

Jesus' death on the Cross has come to mean. The writer of Hebrews, whose identity has never been confirmed, wrote about the transition of the use of animal blood as atonement—to Jesus' blood—once and for all, covering our sins. In Hebrews 9 a little bit of the history of blood sacrifice is reviewed. In verses 19-22:

> When Moses had proclaimed every commandment of the law to all the people, he took the blood of calves, together with water, scarlet wool and branches of hyssop, and sprinkled the scroll and all the people. He said, "This is the blood of the covenant, which God has commanded you to keep." In the same way, he sprinkled with the blood both the tabernacle and everything used in its ceremonies. In fact, the law requires that nearly everything be cleansed with blood, and without the shedding of blood there is no forgiveness.

The writer continues in the next chapter to say,

> It is impossible for the blood of bulls and goats to take away sins *(Hebrews 10:4)*.

> We have been made holy through the sacrifice of the body of Jesus Christ once for all *(Hebrews 10:5)*.

The analogy of being washed in blood for cleaning may seem gory, I know, but it had to be something as powerful as the blood of the sinless God-Man, Jesus, to obstruct the heinous sight of our sin from God's perfect eyes.

I don't think we're ever to understand how it works exactly. I do hope, however, that when we sing about Jesus' blood, we'll find ourselves being thankful for it.

> *Jesus paid it all,*
> *All to Him I owe;*
> *Sin had left a crimson stain,*
> *He washed it white as snow.*[3]

Occasionally you'll find words such as *flood, crimson flood,* and *fountain* used as synonyms for *blood* in songs.

BULWARK

A Mighty Fortress Is Our God
A mighty fortress is our God,
A bulwark never failing;
Our helper He, amid the flood
Of mortal ills prevailing:
For still our ancient foe
Doth seek to work us woe;
His craft and power are great,
And, armed with cruel hate,
On earth is not his equal.[1]

"A Mighty Fortress Is Our God" is said to be "the greatest hymn of the greatest man of the greatest period of German history."[2] Had the word *bulwark* been around in Old Testament days, the psalmist could have used it instead of *refuge* in Psalm 46:1.

God is our refuge and strength, a very present help in trouble.

Bulwark means a hedge of protection, a wall of earth (a levee) against a flood; a fortification. It's also a nautical term, referring to a solid wall around the main deck of a ship for the protection of persons or objects on the deck.

Though the word does not necessarily "sing" well in modern terms, the sound of the word somehow signifies the enormous strength that our God possesses.

CROSS

It took me a long time to write this chapter—not because I didn't know what to write but because I didn't know what *not* to write. The research on the topic of the cross of Christ could take years, for there are too many books, articles, sermons, and even movie scripts written on the Cross's significance to report it all. So I've struggled with the questions: how can I define it—which is what this book is supposed to do—and, more important, how can I ever put it into context for today's culture, which is also a goal of this book?

I decided to start with a touch of history and science. However, this information in no way does the subject justice. If the information seems coldly academic, I apologize.

Death by crucifixion was invented by the Persians but perfected by the Romans.

By the time Jesus came along, crucifixion had almost developed into an art form. There were specialized teams of executioners assigned at each killing. These teams usually included a commanding officer and several soldiers under his authority. The team's job was to bind the prisoner, affix him to the crossbeam with nails in his wrists and feet, and then stay close by until the criminal was dead. This last assignment could account for the fact that often deaths were hastened by the breaking of bones, spears through the body cavity, or sharp blows to the chest. Sometimes smoking fires were built at the foot of the cross to help deprive the victim of oxygen.

The cause of death in a crucifixion could have been blood loss, shock, sepsis, or dehydration. However, the most common theory of the cause of death was asphyxiation. The victim's outstretched arms were required to bear the weight of his body against the gravity that constantly pulled, and as fatigue and muscle spasms set in, inhaling enough air to sustain life became impossible. Depending on the general health of the victim, this process alone could have taken several days. A common belief is that Jesus' death was hastened by a combination of many of these factors, but also it is believed that Jesus gave up the fight to stay alive because of His obedience to His Heavenly Father and His love for us. This is conjecture and/or commentary, however.

Only slaves, rebels, pirates, and especially despised criminals could be crucified under Roman law. Most Roman citizens were exempt from this fate, however, unless a crime of high treason, an offense against the Caesar himself, was pronounced. Ancient Jewish laws did not allow crucifixion as a capital punishment.

So why was Jesus sentenced to death by this method?

Had Jesus' trial ended before the Jewish high priest Caiaphas, His death could have been by stoning or even burning alive since the charge against Him was blasphemy. But, truly, even blasphemy was not a serious enough crime at that time to warrant death, according to the Jews.

That's where the Roman leaders came in. Throughout the night Jesus' guilt was debated, but then it was declared that He had indeed committed an act of treason and would face the Roman execution method. All claims against Jesus were bogus, of course, but the verdict and the sentence were set and carried out in record time.

Now we see that the method of blood sacrifice—and crucifixion was certainly bloody—tied into the Jewish tradition of animal sacrifice (see BLOOD.) The blood of a perfect lamb could atone (see ATONEMENT) for the sins of the worshiper. Perhaps that satisfies the why-was-crucifixion-necessary question, but it's just the tip of the iceberg.

So what does the Cross mean today?

The theology of the Cross is another subject that I could explore here, but my research revealed that this is where speculation and commentary abound. Reporting my findings would probably only raise more questions, such as—Was Christ's execution the only way for us to obtain salvation? Did it have to be crucifixion for His death to have been a fitting sacrifice?

One thing biblical scholars say about Jesus' death on the Cross: It was predicted and dramatized before crucifixion was even regarded as a viable form of execution. Psalm 22, one of David's lyrics, is said to be one of the best examples of prophecy of the impending doom of the Cross.

Here is a comparison of the psalm and the gospel account. The psalm starts out with a cry to God that Jesus quotes verbatim in His dying moments:

My God, my God, why have you forsaken me? *(Psalm 22:1).*

About the ninth hour Jesus cried out in a loud voice, "Eloi, Eloi, lama sabachthani?"—which means, "My God, my God, why have you forsaken me?" *(Matthew 27:46).*

Then the piercing of his hands and feet was predicted.
Dogs have surrounded me; a band of evil men has encircled me, they have pierced my hands and my feet *(Psalm 22:16).*

Though the gospels do not describe the details of the crucifixion this way, we know from history that the hands and feet of the victim were nailed to a wooden beam.

However, concerning one detail of the events surrounding the Cross, the psalmist's words are almost eerie when compared to what actually happened as Jesus was dying.

They divide my garments among them and cast lots for my clothing *(Psalm 22:18)*.

And they crucified him. Dividing up his clothes, they cast lots to see what each would get *(Mark 15:24)*.

Many hymns and modern songs try to make sense of the Cross. Most of them speak of it as a symbol of forgiveness and redemption and shame and glory.

The lyric of "The Old Rugged Cross," one of our most beloved hymns about the Cross, vacillates between fact and feelings, emotions and theology:

> *On a hill far away*
> *Stood an old rugged cross,*
> *The emblem of suff'ring and shame;*
> *And I love that old cross*
> *Where the dearest and best*
> *For a world of lost sinners was slain.*[1]

Then there seems to be poetic resolve in the chorus. It also echoes hope of future reward that the cross was meant to supply:

> *So I'll cherish the old rugged cross,*
> *Till my trophies at last I lay down;*
> *I will cling to the old rugged cross,*
> *And exchange it some day for a crown.*

One of the great new hymns about the Cross, "The Power of the Cross," was written by Keith Getty and Stuart Townend. Here's the chorus:

> *This the pow'r of the cross;*
> *Christ became sin for us;*
> *Took the blame, bore the wrath;*
> *We stand forgiven at the cross!*[2]

As simple as this might sound, I think this chorus gives both weight and definition to this mystery of the cross. Keith writes of their song,

A friend from Westminster Seminary inspired us in the thought of how the cross is not just something in our past providing a way for our salvation, nor is it only providing a secure hope for the future in heaven, but actually it should impact everything we do today. When we come to the cross, we don't just stand there by ourselves—we stand with thousands of people from every tribe and tongue under the same Savior and same grace. Considering how unworthy I am coming to the cross, and finding I am forgiven, how can I then turn and look at others and dishonor them or somehow think I am better than they are?[3]

Bill and Gloria Gaither wrote a great song titled "The Old Rugged Cross Made the Difference":

> *And the old rugged cross made the difference,*
> *In a life bound for heartache and defeat;*
> *I will praise Him forever and ever,*
> *For the cross made the difference for me.*[4]

Gloria relates a story that compelled her to write that lyric with her husband. Here's an excerpt:

Several people invited Bob to church, but he didn't want anything to do with it. He'd attended as a kid, and he'd long ago walked away from the restrictions of that! His wife took the children to church in spite of Bob's opposition, and one day she convinced him to go with her to a concert of a singer named Doug Oldham.

Some months later his wife convinced him to go with her to a revival that was sweeping a nearby college campus. Doug Oldham, the singer he'd heard at the concert, was to sing. The power of prayer was so strong at the beginning of the service that [Bob] knew he had to respond.

Doug saw him coming [down the aisle] and met him there. Together they prayed that God would change Bob from the inside out. He did! And what a change!

For us, it has been the stories told—and lived—by real people that convinced us to stay with the way of the Cross. These stories made their way into a song called "The Old Rugged Cross Made the Difference." For us, it truly has.[5]

There. It's done, but not. I encourage you to continue to dig for meaning and purpose on this subject. And if you do continue to dig, I promise you that you'll never stop discovering something new and wonderful about the cross of Jesus Christ.

DAYS OF ELIJAH

The phrase *Days of Elijah* isn't one we sing often, but it's the title of a very popular song written by Robin Mark. "Days of Elijah" has a wonderful message, especially when you understand the origin and meaning of it. Here's the lyric:

> *These are the days of Elijah,*
> *Declaring the Word of the Lord.*
> *And these are the days of Your servant Moses;*
> *Righteousness being restored.*
>
> *And though these are days of great trials,*
> *Of famine and darkness and sword,*
> *Still we are the voice in the desert crying,*
> *"Prepare ye the way of the Lord."*

Behold, He comes riding on the clouds,
Shining like the sun at the trumpet call.
So lift your voice; It's the year of Jubilee.
And out of Zion's hill salvation comes.

And these are the days of Ezekiel,
The dry bones becoming as flesh,
And these are the days of Your servant, David,
Rebuilding a temple of praise.

And these are the days of the harvest;
The fields are as white in the world.
And we are the laborers in Your vineyard
Declaring the Word of the Lord.

There's no god like Jehovah
There's no god like Jehovah
There's no god like Jehovah
There's no god like Jehovah.[1]

Here are excerpts from an article Robin wrote for *Worship Leader* magazine:

The song is generally and principally a song of "hope." The themes it explores are to do with the fact that [the characters] of Old Testament stories and characters being, either as themselves or by their actions, "types" or "examples" of Christ and the Church. . . . That is, even though they were historical factual people, living in the old covenant days, their actions and characters can be used to teach and represent the character of God under the new covenant, and they continually and repeatedly point to Christ.

First the song came from watching a television show called "Review of the Year" at the end of 1994. This was the year of the Rwandan civil war tragedy, which claimed one million peoples' lives, and also when the first ceasefires in Northern Ireland were declared. On this TV review were a lot of daft stories, happy stories, serious stories, and then absolutely devastating stories like the Rwandan situation. As I watched the review unfold, I found myself despairing about the state of the world and, in prayer, began asking God if He was really in control and what sort of days were we living in.

I felt in my spirit that He replied to my prayer by saying that indeed He was very much in control and that the days we were living in were special times when He would require Christians to be filled with integrity and to stand up for Him just like Elijah did, particularly with the prophets of Baal. "These are Elijah days." Elijah's story is in the Book of Kings (1 Kings 17—19) and you can read how he felt isolated and alone in the culture in which he lived. But God told him to stand up and speak for Him.

We also needed to be a holy and just people, and hence the reference to the "days of your servant Moses," meaning that righteousness and right living were important in all our attitudes and works.

"Days of great trial, of famine, darkness and sword" is a reflection of the apparent times in which we live when still thousands of people die every day from starvation, malnutrition, and war. In the midst of it all we are called to make a declaration of what and whom we believe in.

The second verse refers to the restoration of unity of the body, what Jesus prayed for—"that they may be one even as I and the Father are one" by reference to Ezekiel's prophetic vision of the valley of the dry bones becoming flesh and being knit together (Ezekiel 37). There are lots of interpretations of this picture, but one of a united Church rising up in unity and purpose is a powerful call on us in these days.

The restoration of praise and worship to the Church is represented by "the days of your servant David."

Of course David didn't get to build the structural Temple (that's why the word in the song line is *rebuild*)—that was left to Solomon, his son—but David was used by God to introduce a revised form of worship, praise, and thanksgiving into, first, his little tent, which he pitched around the ark of the covenant (the presence of God), and then the Temple that Solomon his son built.

David's tent was a picture of how Christ would enable us to come right into God's presence, through His sacrifice, and worship openly there.

Finally the "days of the Harvest" point towards what is the purpose of the Christian to go into all the world and make disciples of all nations. By the way, "The fields are as white in the world" is from the King James Version and means they are ripe for harvest.

I hope the explanation is clear. The song is, perhaps, a little complex—but I can assure you that this was not deliberate. I have written lots of simple, straightforward hymns and songs covering lots of themes. This song seems to have been used particularly by God in the ministry of praise and worship, and the themes and pictures it uses seem to have been grasped by God's people all over the world.[2]

Robin Mark lives in Belfast, Ireland, with his wife, Jacqueline, and three children, Catherine, David, and James. He combines an international ministry in praise and worship with the role of director of worship at his home church, CFC, in Belfast; partner in acoustics company F. R. Mark and Associates; and Lecturer in Acoustics in Belfast's Queens University.[3]

 DIADEM

Back in the days of big Hammond organs that were used to accompany congregational singing, "All Hail the Power of Jesus' Name" was a favorite hymn of mine. It was majestic and rousing, and I loved it—both tune versions: "Diadem" and the more familiar "Coronation." Following is the first verse:

> All hail the power of Jesus' name!
> Let angels prostrate fall;
> Bring forth the royal diadem,
> And crown Him Lord of all;
> Bring forth the royal diadem,
> And crown Him Lord of all.[1]

I was clueless as to what *diadem* meant, and it was only recently that I found the origin of the word. It not only clears up the mystery, but it also makes the hymn even more powerful to me.

In just looking at the lyric, it seems that from the other reference to a crown that perhaps *diadem* means the same thing. But sometimes in the Bible a crown is a garland or wreath placed upon the head of the winner of an athletic event.

The *diadem,* however, was reserved for royalty or priesthood. When Moses was ordaining Aaron, his brother, as the first high priest of Israel, the headpiece Moses placed on Aaron's head was a turban that had a band around it with an insignia that signified Aaron's holiness before the Lord (see HOLY).

> Then he placed the turban on Aaron's head and set the gold plate, the sacred diadem, on the front of it, as the LORD commanded Moses *(Leviticus 8:9).*

Exodus 28:36-38 records God's instructions to Moses about the headpiece and the insignia on the turban:

> Make a plate of pure gold and engrave on it as on a seal: HOLY TO THE LORD. Fasten a blue cord to it to attach it to the turban; it is to be on the front of the turban. It will be on Aaron's forehead, and he will bear the guilt involved in the sacred gifts the Israelites consecrate, whatever their gifts may be. It will be on Aaron's forehead continually so that they will be acceptable to the LORD.

The apostle John, in his vision about end times, sees Jesus coming again wearing several headpieces. In Revelation 19:11-13 John writes,

I saw heaven standing open and there before me was a white horse, whose rider is called Faithful and True. With justice he judges and makes war. His eyes are like blazing fire, and on his head are many crowns. He has a name written on him that no one knows but he himself. He is dressed in a robe dipped in blood, and his name is the Word of God.

So a diadem was and will be worn as a badge of royalty.

Chris Machen wrote a song called "Crown Him" that uses diadem in the chorus:

> *Crown Him*
> *Crown Him*
> *Crown Him with the diadem of glory*
> *Crown Him*
> *Crown Him*
> *Crown Him King of kings.*[2]

Chris adds,

My minister of music had done a big Easter pageant for years. In it he had done a traditional banner processional with the various names of Jesus displayed. It was always a highlight. One year he decided to add a new element to the banners being brought forward in the service—crowns! He asked me if I would write a song for that special occasion. The hymn "All Hail the Power of Jesus Name" came immediately to mind.

The royal diadem was a crown reserved for the king. Naturally, this wonderful hymn was speaking of the crown only Jesus could wear. As I thought about crowns, I was reminded of the illustrations of royalty throughout the story of Jesus. The wise men's gifts of gold, frankincense, and myrrh came to mind—gifts fit for a king. Then I thought of the crown of thorns cruelly placed on Jesus brow. It was a crown He didn't deserve; nevertheless, it was one He chose to wear for us.

The Bible describes us in heaven laying our crowns at Jesus feet. One day we and all the angels and believers who have gone before us will all "Crown Him with Many Crowns." These were the images that flooded my thoughts as I wrote. It was actually easy to write thinking of that scene in eternity. Only the king can wear the diadem. And only Jesus will be crowned in heaven. My lyric can't even come close to picturing what it will be like, but one day we will all crown Him.[3]

Not knowing this word's true meaning never made the hymn "All Hail the Power of Jesus' Name" nor these contemporary songs' messages less powerful. Here's a story that illustrates that:

There was a missionary to India named E. P. Scott who discovered a tribe that he believed had never heard the gospel. When Scott told his friends that he felt God leading him to this tribe, the other missionaries begged him not to go. However, Scott went anyway.

After a two-day journey, Scott found the tribe, but he also found himself surrounded by tribesmen who had spears pointed at him. Not knowing what to do, Scott got out his violin and sang and played, "All Hail the Power of Jesus' Name."

By the end of the song, the men had dropped their spears, and many of the tribesmen had tears in their eyes. E. P. Scott remained in the village for two-and-a-half years telling the tribesmen about Jesus.

Sometimes even words we don't understand transcend understanding, and the message of God is received anyway.

EBENEZER

Ask anybody on the street what the word *Ebenezer* means, and most will respond that it's the first name of a famous Charles Dickens character whose last name was Scrooge. Those who sing hymns on a regular basis might give another response but still not know why the word appears in a well-known hymn lyric.

It's too bad that the author of the hymn lyric "Come, Thou Fount of Every Blessing" didn't give a tutorial on what the word *Ebenezer* means. It's found in the second verse of the hymn.

> *Here I raise mine Ebenezer;*
> *Hither by Thy help I'm come;*
> *And I hope by Thy good pleasure*
> *Safely to arrive at home.*[1]

Come to think of it, it might have been nice if he had defined *hither* as well. It simply means "here."

The term *Ebenezer* had its roots in the Old Testament. Samuel, the priest during the transitional time between the judges and the kings of Israel, named a place Ebenezer. Samuel was offering a burnt sacrifice to God as a cry for help against the Philistines. Then in 1 Samuel 7:10 we read,

> While Samuel was sacrificing the burnt offering, the Philistines drew near to engage Israel in battle. But that day the Lord thundered with loud thunder against the Philistines and threw them into such a panic that they were routed before the Israelites.

Then in verses 12 and 13:

> Then Samuel took a stone and set it up between Mizpah and Shen. He named it Ebenezer, saying, "Thus far has the Lord helped us." So the Philistines were subdued and did not invade Israelite territory again.

The name *Ebenezer* literally meant "stone of help." In the hymn it could mean a place to cry for help or a place to give thanks to God.

EL SHADDAI / ALMIGHTY / MIGHTY

She had no control over the disease. It was slowly taking over the healthy tissue in her lungs, which were slowly filling with fluid. The doctors had told us when she was diagnosed that our mother would probably live only three more months. She lived seven. But it was obvious every time I went to visit her that the cancer was unleashing its power upon her, and there was nothing we could do about it.

Absolute power. It felt as if cancer were the supreme commander in my mother's life. Yet I was aware all along that nothing on earth, good or bad, could ever possess such authority. Only God himself is all-powerful, all-controlling, and almighty.

In Hebrew the word *Almighty* was a name God gave himself to reveal another of His attributes. *El Shaddai,* also translated *All-Sufficient One,* was expressed directly from God's mouth to Abram's heart.

> When Abram was ninety-nine years old, the LORD appeared to him and said, "I am God Almighty; [El Shaddai]; walk before me and be blameless" *(Genesis 17:1).*

Isaac sent his son, Jacob, away to make a life of his own by saying,

> May God Almighty [El Shaddai] bless you and make you fruitful and increase your numbers until you become a community of peoples *(Genesis 28:3).*

It's no surprise that Job called upon "El Shaddai" over 20 times in the book chronicling his suffering.

> The Spirit of God has made me; the breath of the Almighty gives me life *(Job 33:4).*

What a testimony that is! And what a statement of faith we make whenever we sing about our God Almighty!

Michael Card and John W. Thompson wrote a song entitled "El Shaddai" in the early 1980s, and it was made famous by Amy Grant. The lyric speaks of God's power, His might, but also His love through the sacrifice of His Son, Jesus.

Following is the chorus of "Almighty," written by Wayne Watson:

> Almighty, most Holy God;
> Faithful through the ages.
> Almighty, most Holy Lord;
> Glorious, Almighty God.[1]

Wayne explains,

> I was writing songs for the "next" project and had twelve or
> thirteen ready to go. I had never written much worship music.
> I always wanted to be true to say what God wanted to say
> through my songs and not force anything. "Almighty" came to
> me on Sunday morning in church. Overwhelming, unhindered
> by humanity, nothing can stand against Him. Thoughts like
> these raced through my head. I heard a descending melody in a
> hymn and sang the word *Almighty* to those three notes.
>
> When the record company guys came to Houston to hear the
> new songs, I pointed out there was one song I was pretty sure
> was not right for the project—"Almighty." They came out of
> the listening room and said, "With all due respect—uh—you're
> crazy!" Glad I listened to them.
>
> And I'm so thankful that God has used this simple song to His
> glory.[2]

 EXALT / EXTOL

The headline read, "Boy Resists Exaltation."

A newspaper story reported that the police department of a small town gave a young boy an award for valor. He had saved his mother's life by dragging her from the flames of their burning house. At the awards ceremony the boy was very embarrassed and reluctant to receive credit for what he had done. When asked why he was so uncomfortable with the accolades, he said, "Well, 'cause I didn't do nothin'."

The boy was being exalted: lifted up, praised, and held in very high regard—in this case, for something he felt deserved no special credit.

Exalt and *extol* are used interchangeably in the Bible over one hundred times. In many instances the words were used in song lyrics in vertical praise to God. In fact, the first time *exalt* appeared in the Bible was in Exodus 15 in a song that's collaboration between Moses and his sister, Miriam. No one knows if this song was written on the spot to praise God for delivering the Israelites from the armies of the pharaoh at the Red Sea, or if Moses and Miriam wrote it beforehand in anticipation of God's deliverance.

Some scholars believe that the word *exalt* could be substituted for the words *lifted up,* used to refer to Jesus being raised up on the Cross.

> Just as Moses lifted up the snake in the desert, so the Son of Man must be lifted up *(John 3:14).*

We tend to think that *lifted up* in this verse is the same as *exalted* and is a prophetic picture of how Jesus would die—lifted up on a cross beam.

Kirk and Deby Dearman wrote a great song of praise called "Above All Else." It speaks to the lifestyle of worship that God intends for us to have.

> *You are exalted, Lord,*
> *Above all else.*
> *We place You at the highest place,*
> *Above all else.*
> *Right now where we stand,*

And ev'rywhere we go
We place You at the highest place,
So the world will know![1]

Kirk writes,

> Right before we wrote "Above All Else" we were living
> as "musicianairies" in Europe. The value of a dollar had
> dropped suddenly, and we had just lost our main source of
> support during the same month. So we had to move from our
> apartment and store belongings in a friend's garage. Not long
> after, the garage flooded in a heavy rainstorm, and our electric
> piano was damaged.
>
> Then the call came to write for a worship project. The only
> piano we could get to was an old, clunky, out-of-tune relic.
> Deby sat down and began to pray for God's heart. She started
> praying and then singing, "You are exalted, Lord, above all else.
> We place You at the highest place, above all else."
>
> I said, "Wait! Sing that again!" She did, and the rest of the song
> was quickly written on the spot. We began singing the song in
> outdoor concerts—most notably in the downtown city square
> of Brussels, Belgium, the capital of Europe, as a declaration of
> God's sovereign lordship over every city and nation.[2]

GLORY

Glory is probably one of the most widely used in words in worship song lyrics and hymns and is perhaps one of the hardest to define. Since the word isn't often spoken in ordinary conversation, we must go back to the time when it was. And even then, the word that we translate as glory came from different roots, and its meaning changed according to the situation.

One of the Hebrew words from which we get glory means literally "heavy in weight." It referred to something that was of great or of weighty importance. It denotes a sense of "awe and reverence." David wrote,

And in his temple all cry, "Glory!" (Psalm 29:9).

In the hymn "Glory to His Name" the chorus uses *glory,* I believe, in this context.

> *Glory to His name,*
> *Glory to His name.*
> *There to my heart was the blood applied,*
> *Glory to His name.*[1]

Weight is given here to Jesus' name.

There are other Hebrew, Aramaic, and Greek words that are translated *glory* as well. And we also have a derivative of the word: *glorious*.

Before David died, he knew that Solomon, his son, would succeed him on the throne and that Solomon would be the one to build a permanent temple on the site where the tabernacle had been (see TABERNACLE/TEMPLE). As this announcement was being made and the people were asked to make offerings to help build the Temple, David offered up a prayer in which the word glorious appears.

Now, our God, we give you thanks, and praise your glorious name *(1 Chronicles 29:13).*

Many times the word *glory* or *glorious* is used to express the inexpressible. This is a place where the word takes a turn away from the definition of reverence for and moves toward the revelation of the nature of God. Often the word as it refers to God simply means to give an accurate accounting of who God is—so that when we "live for the glory of God," we just stand back, get out of the way, and let God do what He does naturally so the world can see Him authentically.

Bill and Gloria Gaither's song "All the Glory Belongs to Jesus" fits this definition well.

> All the glory belongs to Jesus;
> All the praise belongs to Him.
> All that I am or ever hope to be,
> All the glory belongs to Him.[2]

During Jesus' famous after-dinner speech the night before His death, He used the word *glory:*

> I will do whatever you ask in my name, so that the Son may bring glory to the Father *(John 14:13).*

Here it perhaps means to give credit or praise or refers back to an earlier interpretation of giving an accurate accounting of who He is.

It's safe to say that the word *glory* is not sufficient in describing God, His appearances (as Jesus at Bethlehem and in the Second Coming), or the praise due Him. However, sometimes it's the only word we can think of that comes close.

Many churches sing what is known as the "Gloria Patri," which dates back to the second century.

> *Glory be to the Father, and to the Son,*
> *And to the Holy Ghost:*
> *As it was in the beginning,*
> *Is now and ever shall be,*
> *World without end. Amen. Amen.*[3]

This is often called a doxology, which is defined as a "song of praise."

In some places in the New Testament *glory* refers to "a spectacular appearance," as in the narrative of Jesus' birth in the Gospel of Luke referring to the revelation to the shepherds outside Bethlehem:

> And, lo, the angel of the Lord came upon them, and the glory of the Lord shone round about them: and they were sore afraid *(Luke 2:9, KJV).*

Later, speaking of His Second Coming, Jesus says,

> At that time the sign of the Son of Man will appear in the sky, and all the nations of the earth will mourn. They will see the Son of Man coming on the clouds of the sky, with power and great glory *(Matthew 24:30).*

Here, too, it means "splendor" or "a breath-taking spectacle," but it may encompass all of the aforementioned definitions—awe, reverence, and revelation of His true self.

In the Babbie Mason and Donna Douglas chorus to "In All of His Glory", the writers define *glory* within the lyric itself as "splendor and grace" and "majesty."

> *And there He was*
> *In all of His glory.*
> *The promise of God,*
> *In all of His glory.*
> *Beautif'lly arrayed*
> *In splendor and grace,*
> *Clothed in majesty.*
> *There He was,*
> *In all of His glory![4]*

Babbie writes about *glory:*

You and I were created and called to make the beauty and greatness of God known in the whole earth. Our reason for existing is to bring attention to God and point all the nations to Him.

As I ponder these thoughts, I am one of 1,432 passengers aboard the *MS Zaandam,* a luxury cruise liner in the Holland America fleet of ships. I have taken this cruise to the state of Alaska on a number of occasions, but I never tire of it. Our itinerary takes us from Seattle, Washington, up through the Canadian province of British Columbia, to the vast, beautiful land of the midnight sun.

On this balmy afternoon in July, everywhere I look I see God on display. Everything in Alaska is big. The water, the sky, the mountains, the fish, the birds, the animals are massive in Alaska. And I have often described the state as a place where God is "showing off." I witness first-hand God on display, God showing off, God, in all of His glory.

When my co-writer Donna I. Douglas and I wrote the song, "In All of His Glory," we desired to compose a song that contained the message and the story of the gospel. Within the length of the song we aimed to tell the story of the birth, life, death, burial, resurrection, and the coming again of our Lord Jesus Christ. The song, to our amazement, has proven to be one that has lasted long past its initial recording. The lyric is descriptive and inspiring. The melody is memorable and easy to sing. But beyond that, the message of the song—the message of the gospel—is timeless, changeless, and compelling. After all, the gospel message remains the greatest story ever told.

Imagine how it was that first Christmas morning: God, in the flesh, a bouncing baby boy. There in a manger filled with hay and wrapped in swaddling clothes lay the gift to every man, the Baby Jesus, the miracle of miracles, God come to earth.

There He was one day at high noon beside a well in Samaria where He revealed himself as the Living Water to a woman whose life had grown severely parched by the harsh winds of life. Picture Him on a stormy night as He taught His dear friend

Peter to walk on water during a faith adventure out on the high seas.

There He was, that dark day, the ninth hour, hung high and stretched wide on a cruel Roman cross. The King of Kings, the Savior of the World, the sacrifice for sins was mocked, beaten, and crucified until He breathed His last breath, died, and was buried. But after three days He rose again as Victor over death, hell, sin, and the grave, becoming the ultimate sacrifice for sin and reuniting man and God once and for all.

To see God in all of His glory, you do not have to look very far. Just look around. Savor the moment the next time you bite into a vine-ripened tomato, a sweet peach, or a slice of cool watermelon so sweet that the juice runs down your arm. Then remember to thank God, "Who richly provides all things for us to enjoy" *(1 Timothy 6:17).*

Look beyond. Make an effort to rise early and watch the sun come up on a brand-new day, and remember Psalm 118:24—"This is the day that the LORD has made. We will rejoice and be glad in it." Set an appointment to be with Him for the evening sunset when He paints the sky with orange, fuchsia, and magenta. Then remember Psalm 113:3—"From the rising of the sun to the setting of the same, the name of the LORD is to be praised."

Look upward. Sing a song of praise the next time you catch a glimpse of the Big Dipper or the tail of a shooting star as it trails across a navy blue night sky. Then recall, "The heavens declare the glory of God" *(Psalm 19:1).*

Look inward and thank God for His Son, our hope, for He is "Christ in you, the hope of glory" (Colossians 1:27). Then look in the mirror. For God, in all of His glory, is pleased to dwell in you. Just as the unforgettable landscape of Alaska's vast, great land displays how big and beautiful God is, even more He is pleased to allow His glory to be revealed in you. Pay attention. Don't miss Him. Look for an opportunity. God, in all of His glory, longs to show how great He is through you.

The old gospel song "A New Name in Glory" uses the word *glory* as a "synonym for heaven," as does the beloved Christmas carol "Angels, from the Realms of Glory."[5]

Glory and *glorious* are no doubt words of weight that should be used carefully and interpreted accurately.

GRACE

The elegant movements of a dancer; the prayer of thanksgiving before a meal; the allowance for delayed payment; a generous and forgiving spirit—all of these describe grace. But the grace that we sing about is far more than these. The grace of the Old Testament was having the favor of God because of faith or rightness with Him.

Noah found grace in the eyes of the Lord *(Genesis 6:8).*

As with so many biblical concepts, grace became something brand new when Jesus came.

And the child grew and became strong; he was filled with wisdom, and the grace of God was upon him *(Luke 2:40).*

Looking back on the life of Christ he had just witnessed, John admitted,

> The law was given through Moses; grace and truth came through Jesus Christ *(John 1:17)*.

Paul takes it from there. Recognizing that he was a true recipient of grace, therefore understanding the unearned and undeserved favor of God, he knew that this kind of grace would forever change humanity's relationship with God. The event that would bring it to us was the giving of the life of His Son for those who could not, would not, ever be worthy of it. One of Paul's most quotable verses is one that has defined now our reconciliation with God

> It is by grace you have been saved, through faith—and this not from yourselves, it is the gift of God—not by works, so that no one can boast *(Ephesians 2:8-9)*.

In his letter to the Romans, Paul keeps our salvation far separate from our ability to achieve it. And this truly defines grace.

> Very rarely will anyone die for a righteous man, though for a good man someone might possibly dare to die. But God demonstrates his own love for us in this: While we were still sinners, Christ died for us *(Romans 5:7-8)*.

An acrostic that I learned as a kid is a good way to remember the definition and the beauty of grace.

G God's

R Riches (or Redemption)

A At

C Christ's

E Expense

I also learned about grace in hymns such as "Grace Greater than Our Sin."

> *Marvelous grace of our loving Lord,*
> *Grace that exceeds our sin and our guilt,*
> *Yonder on Calvary's mount outpoured,*
> *There where the blood of the Lamb was spilt.*

> *Grace, grace, God's grace,*
> *Grace that will pardon and cleanse within;*
> *Grace, grace, God's grace,*
> *Grace that is greater than all our sin.*[1]

Not only did I learn about grace, but also I'm pretty sure I learned to sing harmony with the uncomplicated alto part to this hymn.

Probably the most beloved and definitive song about grace is none other than John Newton's "Amazing Grace."

> *Amazing grace! How sweet the sound*
> *That saved a wretch like me!*
> *I once was lost but now am found,*
> *Was blind but now I see.*

> *'Twas grace that taught my heart to fear,*
> *And grace my fears relieved;*
> *How precious did that grace appear*
> *The hour I first believed!*
>
> *Through many dangers, toils and snares*
> *I have already come;*
> *'Tis grace hath brought me safe thus far,*
> *And grace will lead me home.*[2]

The author, John Newton, lived much of his life as a hardened slave trader. But one day he recognized and accepted the undeserved favor of God. It forever changed his life and those of us who read his story and sing his songs.

In his final years, Newton considered retiring from the pastorate he had held for many years in a church in London. Finally, in failing health, he is reported to have said, "My memory is nearly gone, but I remember two things: that I am a great sinner, and that Christ is a great Savior."

In his most famous song, the grace that Newton found was responsible for his salvation, his relief from fear, his deliverance from life's obstacles, and his entrance into heaven.

HOLY / HOLINESS

Have you ever felt alone in a crowd? Maybe you were among people you didn't know or you felt out of place among people you did know. Still you felt separate. Different.

The basic definition of the word *holy* means "set apart" or "different," although it doesn't necessarily imply a sense of loneliness. Its broader translation is "separated for God's purposes."

But the use of this word and its derivative, *holiness,* can get confusing at times since in the Scriptures it's used to describe God and His nature, humans and their character, and places that are consecrated for God's purpose.

The first mention of holiness in the Bible is the pronouncement of the seventh day of creation being holy.

And God blessed the seventh day and made it holy, because on it he rested from all the work of creating that he had done *(Genesis 2:3)*.

Then there were places declared holy.

"Do not come any closer," God said. "Take off your sandals, for the place where you are standing is holy ground" *(Exodus 3:5)*.

Thus the definition of a day or a place being "set apart for God's purposes" fits here.

Geron Davis uses the word *holy* to designate a place separated for God's special purpose in his song "Holy Ground."

> *We are standing on holy ground,*
> *And I know that there are angels all around.*
> *Let us praise Jesus now;*
> *We are standing in His presence*
> *On holy ground.*[1]

In their song "Firm Foundation," Nancy Gordon and Jamie Harvill refer to God's Word as *holy*. Much like holy ground, this sets the Bible apart purely to convey God's message.

> *Jesus, You're my firm foundation,*
> *I know I can stand secure.*
> *Jesus, You're my firm foundation,*
> *I put my hope in Your holy Word,*
> *I put my hope in Your holy Word.*[2]

Nancy Gordon writes,

> I experienced holiness before I knew the word *holy.* I was attending a summer music camp as a guest with my friend when I was nine years old. I can still hear the music; I can still hear the words to the song "He's Everything to Me," by Ralph Carmichael.
>
> I didn't want the song to end. I thought everyone was feeling what I was. As I look back now, I know I was experiencing God, and He was speaking to me.
>
> Over forty years later, I've learned the truth of that song through His Word, the Bible. It can be trusted time and time again.
>
> Theologians can describe *holy* with bigger words, loftier thoughts, but I prefer the nine-year-old version that I later wrote into a song: "I put my hope in Your holy word; I put my hope in Your holy Word."[3]

As *holiness* refers to God, it means perfection, purity of heart and action, total absence of evil or malice. It seems that Moses was the first to declare God holy in his and Miriam's famous song of deliverance:

> Who among the gods is like you, O Lord? Who is like you— majestic in holiness, awesome in glory, working wonders?" *(Exodus 15:11).*

God declares himself holy in one of the psalms of David:

> Once for all, I have sworn by my holiness—and I will not lie to David *(Psalm 89:35)*.

Even God's name was proclaimed holy. David, as he was passing the crown of Israel to his son Solomon, declared,

> O LORD our God, as for all this abundance that we have provided for building you a temple for your Holy Name, it comes from your hand, and all of it belongs to you
> *(1 Chronicles 29:16)*.

In his vision of God, Isaiah uses *holy* as a description of the Lord's perfection and also as an exclamation of awe.

One of the angels in Isaiah's vision says,

> Holy, holy, holy is the LORD Almighty; the whole earth is full of his glory *(Isaiah 6:3)*.

This sentiment is repeated in Revelation 4:8 and is the basis for the hymn "Holy, Holy, Holy."

This is much like Moses' reaction when he had a close encounter with God. Moses expressed awe in the presence of God's holiness, but he also expressed fear as well.

> Moses hid his face, because he was afraid to look at God *(Exodus 3:6)*.

Claire Cloninger and David Clydesdale wrote of God's holiness, His awe-inspiring perfection in their song "Holy Is He."

> Holy is He, and great is His glory;
> Holy is He and worthy of our praise.
> I stand in His presence amazed,
> And crown Him with worship and praise.
> Holy is He, holy is He, holy is He.[4]

Claire relates an early experience that put her in touch with God's holiness:

> I think my first awareness of God's holiness occurred during an evening prayer service at church camp in the piney woods of north Louisiana when I was twelve years old.
>
> I've always been pretty much of a talker. Being silent and contemplative did not come naturally for me. That summer at camp the most important thing in the world to me was being with my friends, giggling and talking—talking and giggling.
>
> But one night we met for prayer in a beautiful outdoor pavilion, and God got my attention. Our speaker that night was the camp leader who had a powerful, deep, and almost musical speaking voice. I wasn't listening to what he was trying to say to us kids that particular night, however. I was much too preoccupied with my friends.

God didn't let that stop Him, though. He put on a light show in the black sky that night that silenced our whispers. He flung a bolt of lightning out on the darkness, followed by a crack of thunder. And the congregation fell silent. The overhead lights in the pavilion flickered and went completely black. All giggling ceased.

I believed then, as I do now, that the Lord orchestrated that intrusion into my preteen preoccupations. And he got my attention. That night He used a brief but noisy thunderstorm to open my heart to his awesomeness. He used a room left in darkness to shine a light into my spirit. He set me apart for himself. And as the thunder died down and the rain became a drizzle, in the darkness I could feel His presence, warm and safe and near.

Though Mr. Jenkins continued to speak, it seemed that the only voice I heard was the voice of God himself. In that brief service a holy silence fell within my twelve-year-old heart.

I can't remember a word I heard with my ears that night, but in my heart I heard the Lord say, "Come away with me. There are things I want to say to you."

Now, all these years later, I know the sound of my Father's voice well. I recognize a holy moment when it falls on me, and I wait expectantly to hear from Him.

I've written many lyrics that I can trace to that night at church camp when I was twelve. Here is one of them.[5]

> You called me to be holy,
> And I didn't understand
> 'Cause holy is a long way
> From who I really am.
> But you told me just to trust you,
> To open up my heart
> Then silently you filled me
> With everything you are.
>
> You're the heartbeat of holiness.
> That's who you are.
> You lifted my loneliness
> And set me apart.
> Your voice in the silence
> Opened a door
> To your heartbeat of holiness, Lord.[6]

Louie Giglio and Chris Tomlin write about the perfection—the holiness of the Lord—in a song "Holy Is the Lord."

Louie writes about holiness:

The word *holy* conveys moral purity—and God is the very definition of *pure*—but the word also implies "set apart." When we say God is holy, we are saying that He is not like any other thing. God is "other" (You could say He is completely unique—

uniquely unique.) He is unsurpassed in beauty and worth, forever and always the greatest thing in existence. There is no one like Him—never has been and never will be.[7]

Holiness also applies to humanity. Its synonym, especially as written in the New Testament epistles, is *sanctification.* It still means dedicated or separated for God's use.

Before Jesus came, the holiness of humanity was supposedly measured by adherence to the law. In a reflection of God's purity, He gave humans a sort of "code of holiness."

However, after Jesus came, the definition of holiness changed somewhat. Even though the code was still encouraged, the power to adhere to these laws was commuted through Christ's blood. Paul starts his letter to the Romans with an encouragement to be holy. But he puts a new spin on the word as something that only God himself can attain in us.

> The gospel he promised beforehand through his prophets in the Holy Scriptures regarding his Son, who as to his human nature was a descendant of David, and who through the Spirit of holiness was declared with power to be the Son of God by his resurrection from the dead: Jesus Christ our Lord. Through him and for his name's sake, we received grace and apostleship to call people from among all the Gentiles to the obedience that comes from faith. And you also are among those who are called to belong to Jesus Christ" *(Romans 1:2-6).*

Here holiness is akin to "obedience, but still through the power given to us through Jesus."

And Peter gives the same admonition, even adding a quote from the Old Testament passage recorded in Leviticus:

As obedient children, do not conform to the evil desires you had when you lived in ignorance. But just as he who called you is holy, so be holy in all you do; for it is written: "Be holy, because I am holy" *(1 Peter 1:14-16).*

The next time you feel lonely while in a crowd, ask yourself if it's because you are being set apart for God's purposes. Your loneliness may be the process of holiness being fulfilled in you. If it is, then it's time to praise God!

HOLY SPIRIT

If you look up *Holy Spirit* in a Bible dictionary or commentary, you'll find it defined as "the third Person of the Trinity" joining the Father and the Son. For me, that definition leaves a lot of unanswered questions. Where is the Holy Spirit explained in the Bible? Who is He? How does He work?

One of the dictionaries I own describes *Holy Spirit* in much the same way as other dictionaries do. However, it adds that the Holy Spirit is "the existence of God as a purely spiritual being" and goes beyond the limits of human understanding. I almost stopped reading right there. I'm human, with all the limitations that implies, so how can I ever catch a glimpse of what the term *Holy Spirit* means? I kept searching.

In the Old Testament, the Holy Spirit was described as "the breath of God" or "a spiritual wind." David had felt Him and knew that He was an impalpable sense of God's presence. In Psalm 51:11 David asks God,

> Do not cast me from your presence or take your Holy Spirit from me.

Though impossible to see or touch, the Holy Spirit had power that could be witnessed with all senses. It seems He is the same "breath of God" who parted the Red Sea as the children of Israel were escaping the wrathful approach of Pharaoh's army. In that day the evidence of the Holy Spirit's power was indeed something that could be seen.

As with all things after Jesus' coming, the New Testament references to the Holy Spirit take on new meaning. Jesus prayed at the Last Supper that the Holy Spirit would teach, bring to remembrance, bear witness, and convict of sin those He was leaving behind.

At Pentecost, after Jesus' resurrection and ascension, the "breath of God" seemed actually to enter human souls with specific functions: to give power (Acts 1:8), to inspire (2 Peter 1:21), to call (Acts 13:2), to send out (Acts 13:4), to intercede with the Father (Romans 8:26).

Not all of my questions about the Holy Spirit have been answered. I still cannot explain Him, because He is so visceral. He can be felt and experienced as God's power living in me and all around me, and just as real as those things I sense otherwise.

Gene Mims, senior pastor of Judson Baptist Church, Nashville, and author of *The Kingdom-Focused Church,* once compared a person without the Holy Spirit to an empty glove. Without the hand inside to fill it and give it power, the glove has no direction, no purpose, no "life."

David Huntsinger and the late Dottie Rambo wrote a song to the Holy Spirit, bidding Him come in power to a place of worship.

> *Holy Spirit, Thou art welcome in this place.*
> *Holy Spirit, Thou art welcome in this place.*
> *Omnipotent Father of mercy and grace,*
> *Thou art welcome in this place.*[1]

David adds,

> On a gut level, the Spirit is to me the glue of my life, my comfort and guide. Where would we be without God's spirit, who, according to all theological traditions, convicts us and directs us to Christ?[2]

HOPE

My hope is built on nothing less
Than Jesus' blood and righteousness.
I dare not trust the sweetest frame,
But wholly lean on Jesus' name.

On Christ the solid Rock I stand,
All other ground is sinking sand;
All other ground is sinking sand.[1]

Hope is a four-letter word that has profound meaning to believers.
As a noun, *hope* is considered a gift of the Holy Spirit (see HOLY
SPIRIT). One Bible dictionary says that hope is "not merely
expectations and desires as the world might see it, but involves
trust, confidence and refuge in God." Another dictionary said that

hope is the "certainty that what God has done for us in the past guarantees our place in what God will do in the future."

Among the qualities that Christians possess, Paul lists hope right up there with faith and love. (See 1 Corinthians 13:13.)
The word was also used in the New Testament as a synonym for Jesus. When Paul is writing to the church at Colossae, he uses the term "hope of glory" to describe the evidence of Christ in the saints.

Christ in you, the hope of glory *(Colossians 1:27)*.

He calls Jesus "our hope" in the opening statements of his first letter to Timothy.

In Titus 2 Paul calls Jesus the "blessed hope" as he describes the Second Coming of Christ.

Peter writes in his first letter to the church,
Praise be to the God and Father of our Lord Jesus Christ! In his great mercy he has given us new birth into a living hope through the resurrection of Jesus Christ from the dead *(1 Peter 1:3)*.

It seems to me that hope is more about the reality of Jesus Christ than any desire or earthly expectation we might have.

The writer of Hebrews calls this hope the "anchor of the soul" (Hebrews 6:19). I don't think I can describe hope in more concrete terms than that.

It reminds me of a hymn I grew up singing. Ruth Caye Jones wrote "In Times like These" in 1943 in the middle of World War II, but it still rings of hope today.

The anchor of the soul—hope—is one of my most cherished possessions.

HOSANNA

We use the word *hosanna* in Easter pageants—especially in the Triumphal Entry scenes. And the word has been used as an expression of praise in almost every song that includes this word. However, the original use of the term was a desperate cry for help. Psalm 118 is tagged as a song of thanksgiving, but toward the end the psalmist suddenly cries out in verses 25-26,:

> LORD, save us! [or Hosanna!] Blessed is he who comes in the name of the LORD.

This exclamation became part of Jewish worship at the Feast of Tabernacles. Psalms 113-118—called the Hallel—was chanted by one of the priests during this seven-day celebration. "Hosanna; blessed is he who comes in the name of the LORD" was a recitation that the people shouted with the priest as they waved palm and willow branches. The last day of the Feast of Tabernacles was even called "the great Hosanna."

It's from this Psalm that the citizens of Jerusalem got their cry the Sunday that Jesus rode through their palm-branch-covered streets:
Hosanna to the Son of David! Blessed is He who comes in the name of the Lord! Hosanna in the highest heaven! (*John 12:13*).

Going from a desperate cry for help to an expression of praise may mean that when Jesus rode through the Jerusalem streets, He was finally recognized as the Savior they had waited for. In less than a week He would offer himself up as a sacrifice so that we could be saved from our own sins.

"Hosanna," a song written by Brenton Brown and Paul Baloche, expressed the desperation and the praise.

> *Hosanna! Hosanna!*
> *You are the God who saves us,*
> *Worthy of all our praises;*
> *Hosanna! Hosanna!*
> *Come, have Your way among us,*
> *We welcome You here, Lord Jesus.*[1]

Brenton adds,
We love the idea of singing the word *Hosanna* again. I love the history of that word. It originally meant "Save us, God!" but then it came to mean "Thank you, God" or "Praise you, God." I like that,

because it seems to be a good picture of what our lives are like when we come to the Lord. We meet Him as Savior, and we often leave praising and saying, "Thank you." So that's what the word *hosanna* means, and we try to get that into the lyric of the song.

> *Hosanna!*
> *You are the God who saves us*
> *Worthy of all our praises.*

When we were writing that song, we had a split screen in our minds. On the left side we had just our families coming into church being called into corporate worship. At the same time we were imagining the entrance of Jesus into Jerusalem, riding on a donkey. God was coming into their neighborhood. Jesus is recognized perhaps for the first time in His ministry as the coming King Messiah, the promised King of Israel who would restore Israel.

If you jump back to the other side of the screen, that's what's happening when we get together as God's people when we enthrone Him on our praises and acknowledge Him as King. He comes into our midst and changes things and saves us, and we leave with worship. I like the idea of worship as a response to all that God does—the saving action of God in our lives.

Just as Israel longed for the return of their King, we long for God's return to our lives to take us out of exile and restore us to Him.[2]

Since we have now found Jesus to be our salvation (See SAVIOR), our use of this word can be another articulation of praise. However, we can still remember it in its original context and use it as a cry of deliverance from pain and suffering.

IMMANUEL / EMMANUEL

I think I understand fear. I've experienced it a few times in my life. My first taste of fear of the unknown—of impending doom— occurred when I broke the tip of the blade on my father's cherished pocketknife. He had gotten the knife in Europe during World War II. He kept it razor sharp, periodically rubbing the blade across a rock he called a "flint."

I found the knife one day lying unattended on my father's dresser, calling to me to possess it. Somehow in the next few moments I managed to open the blade and stick it into the bark of a pine tree in the backyard, breaking off the tip in the process. I knew immediately that I was a goner. My father would be furious, and I would be punished most severely.

In Bible times, believe it or not, the name *Immanuel* was spoken to chase away all fear of the unknown and a time like this.

It all started with an evil king named Ahaz, who ruled over the southern kingdom of Judah, whose capital was Jerusalem, during the days of Isaiah. An attempt to overtake Jerusalem by the king of the Northern Kingdom, Israel, was thwarted, but an ominous threat still loomed. Apparently the kings of Israel and Syria were going to join forces and try again to conquer the city.

The prophet Isaiah was sent by God to the king to try to calm his fears and perhaps bolster his faith. Isaiah's words were not enough to quiet the king's angst, so God spoke directly to Ahaz:

"Ask the Lord your God for a sign, whether in the deepest depths or in the highest heights."
But Ahaz said, "I will not ask; I will not put the Lord to the test" *(Isaiah 7: 11-12).*

Ahaz was gripped by fear of his enemies and too afraid to ask God's help. So Isaiah spoke for God to the whole nation of Judah. Isaiah proclaims that God would give them a sign anyway:

The Lord himself will give you a sign: The virgin will be with child and will give birth to a son, and will call him Immanuel *(Isaiah 7:14).*

We now know this to be a prophecy concerning the coming of Messiah. However, the sign would not come nor the name spoken again (except briefly in Isaiah 8) for another 700 years.

The next time the name *Immanuel* was spoken, it was again as a sign and recorded by the apostle and gospel writer Matthew. A young man named Joseph was distraught to find out that his fiancé, Mary, was pregnant. She was vowing, however, that she was still a virgin. Finally an angel spoke to Joseph in a dream and assured him that Mary was telling the truth and that the child she was carrying was indeed the long-awaited Messiah. Then Matthew adds,

> All this took place to fulfill what the Lord had said through the prophet: "The virgin will be with child and will give birth to a son, and they will call him Immanuel—which means, 'God with us'" *(Matthew 1:22-23).*

Each time the name *Immanuel* is spoken in Scripture, it's the promise of the sign of God's presence to people who greatly feared what they didn't know and couldn't control—the future. The difference between these two men? Ahaz did not heed the sign and allied himself with an army that would soon overtake him. Joseph, however, recognized and obeyed the voice of the Lord and soon became the legal guardian to the Son of God. Joseph's fears were apparently quelled at that sign of Immanuel.

Immanuel—God with us—is the name that was meant to calm our greatest fears, especially those about our future.

Sometimes the spelling differs—*Emmanuel*—particularly in the King James Version of Matthew's gospel; however, the meaning is identical.

Usually categorized as an advent (a time of waiting) hymn, the song "O Come, O Come Emmanuel" seems to have echoes of longing that the Jews must have been feeling as they waited for their Redeemer (see REDEEM/REDEEMER).

> O come, O come, Emmanuel,
> And ransom captive Israel,
> That mourns in lonely exile here,
> Until the Son of God appear.[1]

As I recall, when my father found the knife, his wrath was not as fierce as I had imagined it would be, but I think I began to understand in my childlike way how uncertainty of the future can bring about paralyzing fear. I'm so glad that I now recognize "the sign" of Immanuel and that God truly is with me!

INCARNATE WORD

You've probably heard the story about the child who was afraid of the dark and began to cry one night at bedtime. The mother encouraged the child by saying, "But God is here right now in this room to protect you," to which the child replied, "Yeah, but I need somebody with skin on him!"

That's what the Incarnate Word is all about. It's God in the flesh. Though the phrase *Incarnate Word* does not appear in Scripture, the concept certainly does.

The apostle John, who was witness to this very fact, wrote,
> The Word became flesh and made his dwelling among us. We have seen his glory, the glory of the One and Only, who came from the Father, full of grace and truth *(John 1:14).*

He was talking about Jesus, of course—the Incarnate Word.

We hear this phrase mostly in songs at Christmastime. One of the verses in the carol "Hark! The Herald Angels Sing" uses the word *incarnate* (see EMMANUEL/IMMANUEL).

> Hail, the Heav'n-born Prince of Peace!
> Hail, the Son of Righteousness!
> Light and life to all He brings,
> Ris'n with healing in His wings.
> Veiled in flesh the Godhead see;
> Hail incarnate Deity,
> Pleased as man with men to dwell,
> Jesus, our Emmanuel.[1]

"O Come, All Ye Faithful" reiterates the concept if not the word in one of its verses.

> Yea, Lord, we greet Thee,
> Born this happy morning;
> Jesus, to Thee be all glory given;
> Word of the Father,
> Now in flesh appearing!
> O come, let us adore Him,
> O come, let us adore Him,
> O come, let us adore Him,
> Christ the Lord.[2]

In the hymn "Come, Thou Almighty King" each part of the Holy Trinity is described in the verses. The first verse is about the Godhead. The second verse describes Jesus.

> *Come, Thou Incarnate Word,*
> *Gird on Thy mighty sword;*
> *Our prayer attend!*
> *Come, and Thy people bless,*
> *And give Thy Word success;*
> *Spirit of holiness,*
> *On us descend.*[3]

Incarnate Word refers to God "with skin on Him."

JEHOVAH / YAHWEH

I have a friend who named herself. That's right—she chose her own name.

She was in a long line of children, and I guess her exhausted mother had run out of names by the time my friend came along. For several years she was called by a cute nickname—and greatly loved, I might add. However, when she was about six years old and it was time for her to start school, she needed a completed birth certificate with a proper name. So every day for a while her mother would give her a list of options to choose from. Nothing suited her. Finally the mother presented a name the little girl liked. The name went on the birth certificate, and we all call her by that name to this day.

Jehovah is one of the first names of God we find in Scripture, and it's one He gave himself. *Yahweh* is the Hebrew original, and *Jehovah* is the English equivalent. The word more formally means "self-existent one," according to those who have tried to translate it. But it comes from a basic Hebrew word that simply means "to be." It can also be translated "I Am."

Do you remember when Moses encountered God for the first time in the inextinguishable fiery bush? It was through the bush that God told Moses to go back to Egypt and get His people out of bondage. Lacking—but surely needing—credentials on which to plead for the Jews' release, Moses asked for a name to put with this voice. "I AM WHO I AM," said God. And that's the essence of the meaning of the name *Jehovah* or *Yahweh*.

Later, after the exodus from Egypt and after Moses came down the second time from Mt. Sinai with the tablets of stone with the Ten Commandments written upon them, the Jews apparently began taking God's laws seriously. Hoping not to repeat the major faux pas they had made with the golden idol, they tried very hard not to disappoint God again. The third commandment, regarding God's name, was one they took to heart:

> Thou shalt not take the name of the LORD thy God in vain; for the LORD will not hold him guiltless that taketh his name in vain *(Exodus 20:7, KJV).*

Because of this commandment, the Israelites did not want to take any chances by using God's name flippantly or loosely. So the name *Jehovah,* or *Yahweh,* which appears in the Bible almost 7,000 times, was never pronounced in the reading-aloud of scripture. Either *Adonai* (see ADONAI), which means "Lord", or *Elohim,* which means "Creator," was substituted. The correct pronunciation, then, was lost in history, because it was not heard spoken aloud again. Scribes tried so hard to adhere to the law that they even began transcribing the word *Yahweh* using only its consonants. So the word looked like this: YHWH.

In 1745 John Hughes and William Williams wrote the great hymn "Guide me, O Thou Great Jehovah." It calls on the Father (Jehovah) to guide, strengthen, and sustain.

> *Guide me, O Thou great Jehovah,*
> *Pilgrim through this barren land;*
> *I am weak, but Thou art mighty;*
> *Hold me with Thy powerful hand;*
> *Bread of heaven, Bread of heaven,*
> *Feed me till I want no more,*
> *Feed me till I want no more.*[1]

In addition to God's self-naming proclamation, the people added suffixes to the name *Jehovah.* These add-ons helped to identify with our great God in more personal and intimate ways. For instance, Hagar, the outcast maidservant of Abram and Sarai, attributed *Jehovah-El Roi* to God.

She gave this name to the LORD who spoke to her: "You are the God who sees me [Jehovah El-Roi]," for she said, "I have now seen the One who sees me" *(Genesis 16:13).*

Jehovah-Jireh, which means "the Lord will provide," is a suffix added by Abraham at the place where he went to sacrifice his only son, Isaac. When God stopped Abraham just before he drew a knife to kill his son, He provided a substitute sacrifice, a ram caught in the thicket. Abraham calls the place "Jehovah-Jireh."

So Abraham called that place The LORD Will Provide *(Genesis 22:14).*

The suffix has since been attributed to God as the provider of all things.

Jehovah-Rapha, also spelled Ropheh, means "God our healer." If you listen carefully to the voice of the LORD your God and do what is right in his eyes, if you pay attention to his commands and keep all his decrees, I will not bring on you any of the diseases I brought on the Egyptians, for I am the LORD, who heals you [Jehovah-Rapha] *(Exodus 15:26).*

Jehovah-Nissi means "The LORD is my Banner (see BANNER).

Jehovah-Shalom means "The LORD is peace." Again, a place was named for God, but then later attributed to the Lord himself (see PEACE).

Jehovah-Raah is "The LORD is my Shepherd," which we all know comes from David's pastoral song, Psalm 23.

Jehovah-Shammah means "God is there," and this was a name in the last verse of the Book of Ezekiel.

There are other suffixes added to *Jehovah*, but the aforementioned ones more often appear in lyrics.

JERUSALEM / NEW JERUSALEM

If there has ever been a center of the universe for Christians and
Jews, it would be the city of Jerusalem. In Deuteronomy 12 God is
said to choose it as "the place."

> You are to seek the place the Lord your God will choose from
> among all your tribes to put his Name there for his dwelling. To
> that place you must go *(Deuteronomy 12:5)*.

Apparently this refers to what is now known as the city of
Jerusalem.

The city itself has had an interesting past. Throughout the Old
Testament, it was the center of worship. David and his armies
captured it, and the king declared that it was the place where the
ark of the covenant would remain. When David's son Solomon built

a permanent Temple there, apparently Jehovah chose to let His presence fill the place. This was more than a stamp of approval, but God set this city apart from all others on earth. Read the exciting account in 1 Kings 8.

Scholars aren't sure who first gave the ancient city its name. It could have its roots with the Jews, since the name ends with a variation of the Hebrew word *shalom,* which means "peace." The Arab word for peace is *salaam,* which may indicate that the name's origin is Arabic. Either way, it implies the definition of the name as "the city of peace."

For Christians, the central events that are the foundations of our faith occurred in Jerusalem. Jesus was crucified there and then arose from the dead there. He ascended back into heaven there. And at Pentecost the Holy Spirit came upon many believers there. The city is also a place that prophecies name as the site of Jesus' Second Coming.

John writes,

> Then I saw a new heaven and a new earth, for the first heaven and the first earth had passed away, and there was no longer any sea. I saw the Holy City, the new Jerusalem, coming down out of heaven from God, prepared as a bride beautifully dressed for her husband. And I heard a loud voice from the throne saying, "Now the dwelling of God is with men, and he will live with them. They will be his people, and God himself will be with

them and be their God. He will wipe every tear from their eyes. There will be no more death or mourning or crying or pain, for the old order of things has passed away" *(Revelation 21:1-4).*

It's this place, the New Jerusalem, that we seem to sing about the most.

There are many people who believe that the "New Jerusalem" refers to the Church as it is now, that "New" is a reference to the covenant that Jesus ushered in at the Cross/Resurrection. They maintain the belief that the "New Jerusalem" is here, now embodied in the Church.

There are others, however, that believe that the "New Jerusalem" is yet to come and that John's vision refers to the end times when Jesus comes back to earth and sets up a reign of peace on earth.

In song, the latter definition is probably more prominent and suggests that it is a heavenly place in which believers will live forever.

The Holy City

Last night I lay a-sleeping,
There came a dream so fair.
I stood in old Jerusalem
Beside the temple there.
I heard the children singing,
And ever as they sang,

Methought the voice of angels
From heaven in answer rang.

Jerusalem! Jerusalem!
Lift up your gates and sing,
Hosanna in the highest!
Hosanna to your King![1]

There are also hymns that speak of this place, Jerusalem, and still in the future sense. Several tunes have been paired with the following lyric, but here are the first two verses:

Jerusalem, My Happy Home

Jerusalem, my happy home!
Name ever dear to me;
When shall my labors have an end,
In joy, and peace, and thee?

Thy saints are crowned with glory great;
They see God face to face.
They triumph still, they still rejoice;
Most happy is their case.[2]

This does not sound like the modern-day city in Israel but, as most texts imply, the New Jerusalem, our ultimate and glorious destination.

 JORDAN

Songwriters have sometimes taken places with ancient biblical and historical significance and used them metaphorically in song lyrics. Jerusalem, Ebenezer, and Gilead are some places I have explored in this book and shown how the lyricists used these poetically to make a point. The word *Jordan,* or *Jordan River,* is another biblical landmark that has been occasionally used in hymns.

The first song that comes to mind referring to a river that flows north to south through Israel and surrounding countries is "On Jordan's Stormy Banks I Stand."

> *On Jordan's stormy banks I stand*
> *And cast a wishful eye*
> *To Canaan's fair and happy land,*
> *Where my possessions lie.*[1]

Mention in Scripture of the river and its fertile valley goes back to Abram. When he and Lot were dividing up their land, Lot chose the most desirable region—that land around the Jordan River—for himself.

> Lot looked up and saw that the whole plain of the Jordan was well watered, like the garden of the Lord *(Genesis 13:10)*.

Indeed, the land around the Jordan River was choice property because of its growing and grazing potential. But the hymn isn't speaking only of lush farmland, is it?

Moving through Scripture, we see that the river becomes even more significant as time passes. After the Israelites had wandered in the wilderness those forty years following their Egyptian exodus, the land they had been longing for and promised lay across the Jordan River from where they had been waiting. It was the Promised Land that God had told them was theirs for the taking. This is what happened when Joshua led the people into their new home:

> Now the Jordan is at flood stage all during harvest. Yet as soon as the priests who carried the ark reached the Jordan and their feet touched the water's edge, the water from upstream stopped flowing. It piled up in a heap a great distance away. . . . So the people crossed over opposite Jericho. The priests who carried the ark of the covenant of the Lord stood firm on dry ground in the middle of the Jordan, while all Israel passed by until the whole nation had completed the crossing on dry ground *(Joshua 3:15-17)*.

Like the parting of the Red Sea forty years earlier, this was another miraculous sign from God that He indeed wanted His chosen people to live abundantly.

The chorus of "On Jordan's Stormy Banks I Stand" brings in the Promised Land reference:

> *I am bound for the Promised Land,*
> *I am bound for the Promised Land;*
> *O who will come and go with me?*
> *I am bound for the Promised Land.*

It is generally thought that this lyric compares Canaan, the Promised Land, to heaven. The *Jordan,* then, is that passage between life and eternal rest believers will find in heaven.

Later in Scripture, however, the Jordan River remains significant through the life of Jesus for another reason.

> At that time Jesus came from Nazareth in Galilee and was baptized by John in the Jordan. As Jesus was coming up out of the water, he saw heaven being torn open and the Spirit descending on him like a dove. And a voice came from heaven: "You are my Son, whom I love; with you I am well pleased" *(Mark 1:9-11).*

This marked the beginning of Jesus' public ministry, so it seems the Jordan was, in fact, His place of crossing over too.

The hymn "Guide Me, O Thou Great Jehovah" refers to the Jordan as not only a cross-over spot but also a treacherous one:

> When I tread the verge of Jordan,
> Bid my anxious fears subside;
> Bear me through the swelling current,
> Land me safe on Canaan's side'
> Songs of praises, songs of praises
> I will ever give to Thee,
> I will ever give to Thee.[2]

So Jordan was in a biblical sense a point of departure, a threshold of decision, or even a barrier to what God wants for His own. Consider your symbolic Jordan. Is there a barrier still between you and His promise? Are you bound for the Promised Land? Do you cast a wishful eye?

KINGDOM

Castles. Moats. Kings and queens. Lord and ladies. Knights of the Round Table.

At least that's what I think of when I hear the word *kingdom.* Maybe you think of a kingdom with Cinderella's castle as the centerpiece.

But the kingdom of God—or kingdom of heaven, as it's translated by Matthew—has very little in common with these images. There is a king, but that's just about as far as the similarities go. The term *kingdom of God* does not appear in the Bible before Jesus himself said it. But it's important that we explore the subject of God's kingdom since it was the central theme of Jesus' ministry. He said so himself.

> I must preach the good news of the kingdom of God to the other towns also, because that is why I was sent (*Luke 4:43*).

Before Jesus, the *Kingdom* references that related to "God's dominion" were all-inclusive. God was the Creator and Sustainer of all things. He, therefore, reigns over it all. The psalmist writes of God,

> The LORD has established his throne in heaven, and his kingdom rules over all *(Psalm 103:19)*.

And then he writes to God,

> Your kingdom is an everlasting kingdom, and your dominion endures through all generations *(Psalm 145:13)*.

However, when Jesus started preaching and teaching about the kingdom of God, the idea naturally took a twist, one that very few understood. Jesus even warned His disciples that it was a "secret."

> When he was alone, the Twelve and the others around him asked him about the parables. He told them, "The secret of the kingdom of God has been given to you" *(Mark 4:10-11)*.

The King James Version of this same passage calls it a "mystery" instead of a "secret." But then in Jesus' Sermon on the Mount, He tells the listeners to seek the kingdom and not to worry about earthly things.

> Seek first his kingdom and his righteousness, and all these things will be given to you as well *(Matthew 6:33)*.

So how would they seek something that was so undefined, secret, and mysterious?

Jesus did try to describe it to them in His own way, sometimes through parables. His illustrations, recorded in all four gospels, indicate that the Kingdom is like seeds (Mark 4:30) and yeast (Luke 13:20-21).

It is a place of feasting (Luke 13:29; 14:15).

Those who may enter it are ones who produce fruit (Matthew 21:43) and are poor of spirit (Luke 6:20).

Jesus said that it's hard for a rich man to enter the kingdom of God (Matthew 19:24) but that it's easy for a child, tax collectors, and prostitutes to enter (Matthew 21:32).

Jesus says the Kingdom belongs even to children (Luke 18:16) and that it requires one's full attention.

> Jesus replied, "No one who puts his hand to the plow and looks back is fit for service in the kingdom of God" *(Luke 9:62).*

Jesus said it was near (Mark 1:15; Luke 10:11) and that it could be seen (Mark 9:1).

But all these metaphors and similes didn't make much sense two thousand years ago. The Jews had been expecting a new king and kingdom, yes; but they were looking for a conqueror-type sovereign. Most of them were looking for a warrior like David or a prophet like Elijah. None of the illustrations that Jesus used for the Kingdom were easy to understand.

However, Jesus finally says that the *kingdom of God* is "within you" (Luke 17:20-22). And there it was. Some of His followers started to get it—His kingdom would be spiritual rather than physical. It would be ushered in by Jesus' death and resurrection and would be evidenced in the lives of the people who would humble themselves before God and would give their lives totally to Him.

I'm not sure the hymn writers were really clear about the kingdom of God, though, as Jesus preached it, since the most popular songs vary widely in their take on the subject. For instance, "I Love Thy Kingdom, Lord" assigns the realm of God as the Church, which wasn't really part of Jesus' teaching.

> *I love Thy kingdom, Lord,*
> *The house of Thine abode,*
> *The church our blest Redeemer saved*
> *With His own precious blood.*[1]

Isaac Watts makes Jesus' kingdom sound more territorial, and the lyric seems to refer to when He comes again rather than His present-day realm.

> *Jesus shall reign where'er the sun*
> *Does his successive journeys run;*
> *His kingdom stretch from shore to shore,*
> *Till moons shall wax and wane no more.*[2]

The hymn I learned in the children's mission organization implies that the Kingdom begins in heaven and will eventually come to earth. This follows Jesus' future reign theme.

> For the darkness shall turn to dawning,
> And the dawning to noonday bright;
> And Christ's great kingdom shall come to earth,
> The kingdom of love and light.[3]

My pastor, Gene Mims, defines the spiritual kingdom of God as "the domain of God in the lives of His people, giving them the power to serve Him wholeheartedly and to live the kind of life Jesus died to give them."[4]

So what's a domain? We all know what a domain name is, right? It's an Internet term. It's a label of identification to define a realm of administrative authority or control. That which God controls can be the all-inclusiveness of all Creation, but in the spiritual definition, His domain is the lives of those people who allow Him to have full authority and control.

LAMB OF GOD

I remember taking my first bite of lobster. I was eight, and my palate was familiar with hamburgers, pizza, and cookies, so the texture and taste of this new thing was not so pleasant. I think I put on a smile for the hostess who had asked me to try it, and then I spit it out as soon as I could. Little did I know that lobster was—and still is—a delicacy I would someday come to enjoy.

In the ancient Hebrew world, meat was not often served. In fact, the serving of any meat at a meal was reserved for special occasions. So a taste of lamb was a rare treat. Lamb was the delicacy—the lobster or caviar of the day—especially if it was from a *perfect* lamb.

This made lamb special and therefore expensive—the perfect sacrifice—something rare, costly, and pure.

Throughout the Bible, beginning with Abel in Genesis 4:4, animal (blood) sacrifice was required of a worshiper (see BLOOD). Even into the New Testament, the spilling of blood from a perfect animal was considered extravagant, but it was an essential gift if one was to give God a proper offering.

In Leviticus the Law tells us that sin could be wiped away by the sacrifice of a female lamb. The blood of a lamb could restore fellowship with God. If you want gory details about how the animals were to be killed and laid on the altar, read the first few chapters in Leviticus. The point is this: the slaughter of a pure animal could somehow cover the sin that the people had committed and reinstate the worshiper to a right relationship with God.

In a more abstract way, is that not what Jesus' blood did for us?

When John the Baptist introduced Jesus of Nazareth to a crowd by saying "Look, the Lamb of God, who takes away the sin of the world!" (John 1:29), it was not a foreign concept. At least the "lamb" part was not new to them.

On the day of Jesus' execution, the perfect sacrifice—the Lamb of God—would be made. Blood would be spilt. Rare and precious was the sacrifice, for this was the only truly begotten Son of God.

When the apostle John wrote the Book of Revelation, he referred to

Jesus as the Lamb but never the Lamb of God. Scholars don't know why exactly, except that perhaps John was referring to the time when Jesus comes to earth again, not as a costly sacrifice—like a lamb to slaughter, as Isaiah put it—but as a victorious Sovereign.

We love to sing the chorus of Dennis Jernigan's song "You Are My All in All."

> *Jesus, Lamb of God,*
> *Worthy is Your name!*
> *Jesus, Lamb of God,*
> *Worthy is Your name!*[1]

Dennis says,

> When I think about my own life and all God has done to set me free, I cannot help but be drawn to the term "Lamb of God." It was at a 2nd Chapter of Acts concert in 1981 when the concept of the perfect sacrifice paying the debt of my sin made perfect sense to me. I had grown up in church—struggling with same-sex attraction—and suddenly here I was at a Christian concert needing to hear God, and all I could do was weep as it dawned on me that Jesus, that perfect sacrificial Lamb, had taken my vile, wicked, willful sin upon himself and paid my debt in full.

> That night I walked away from my old life and walked toward that Lamb. It would be only a few short years later that God would call me to share of my deliverance in a very public way, and that scared me to death. But I learned I could trust the

Lamb, because He saw my life as worth His own. How could I not follow after that kind of love?

One morning while in prayer, the Lord came to remind me of that Lamb's sacrifice and of how His love had drawn me to follow after Him with all my heart and that, regardless of my past experience, present temptations, or any circumstances, knowing Him intimately was worth everything.

All I could think of was how much freedom I had found as a result of His sacrifice and of how many others needed to hear of such a great love. "You Are My All in All" was born during that time of prayer while simply telling the Lord what His great sacrificial love meant to me.[2]

Greg Nelson and Phill HcHugh refer to the Lamb of God in their beautiful song "Lamb of Glory."

> *Precious Lamb of glory,*
> *Love's most wondrous story,*
> *Heart of God's redemption of man,*
> *Worship the Lamb of glory.*[3]

Greg writes,

My family and I chose to visit Disney World in August one year. Oddly, the searing memory of the 98-degree heat index pales in comparison to remembering so vividly losing our then four-year-old son, Benjamin, in the crowd. There is no describing the crippling terror that came over me. I still can't get my mind around that numbing feeling of panic, fear, blame, hurt, and a confluence of other emotions. Ben came back into view after a mere few minutes, but both my wife and I were traumatized for the rest of the trip.

This is how intensely we love our children. Do anything to us, but leave our children alone. This incident is one way for me to wrap my head around "The Lamb of God."

I'm not a theologian, but it's my understanding that God planned for our salvation before the foundations of the earth. He would offer for all humanity the ultimate sacrifice of His only Son Jesus—His lamb—on a Roman cross. Smarter people than I use words like *propitiation, atonement, redemption, justification by faith,* the *sanctifying work of the cross,* and stuff like that. It makes my head swim. They can tell you how God was feeling and what it all means. I'm sixty as of this writing, and I still can't grasp the enormity and its meaning. I have no earthly idea what God is thinking or what His ways are, but the momentary loss of my son gave me but a glimpse.

Sometimes the simplest message is the strongest message. Phill McHugh and I wrote "Lamb of Glory," which contains our simple understanding of the Lamb of God. There would be a sacrifice, and blood would flow to pay sin's price.[4]

LILY OF THE VALLEY /
ROSE OF SHARON

I am a rose of Sharon, a lily of the valleys.
(Song of Solomon 2:1)

Oh, the poetry of King Solomon! If you can read his Song of
Songs—or Song of Solomon—without blushing, you're unlike most
of us. There are references to love that border on lustful language,
but the metaphors, we're told, are deep sentiments from the heart
of one who loves another. It reads almost like a play with lines
spoken from "the lover" and from "the beloved" and "the friends"
(or the chorus) as in an ancient Greek drama.

Scholars tell us that this love song—or collection of love songs—is
an allegory of the love between God and Israel or between Christ
and the Church, although there are no references or quotes from
this Old Testament book in the New Testament.

Isaiah mentioned the beauty of places like Carmel and Sharon (Isaiah 35:1), and some say that these two references—the one from Solomon and one from Isaiah—to their beauty must mean that they were stunning. A rose in Sharon, then, would be beauty upon beauty.

Some think that the *lily* Solomon refers to is the "Madonna lily," which is rare but beautiful.

The two names *Rose of Sharon* and *Lily of the Valley* have been attributed to Christ as though Solomon's song was prophetic, describing the not-yet-come Savior in terms that reflected His unique presence as "God with us" (See EMMANUEL/IMMANUEL).

Here's a great old hymn where two slightly obscure names attributed to Christ are used (see MORNING STAR):

> *I've found a friend in Jesus,*
> *He's everything to me;*
> *He's the fairest of ten thousand to my soul;*
> *The Lily of the Valley,*
> *In Him alone I see*
> *All I need to cleanse and make me fully whole.*
> *In sorrow He's comfort,*
> *In trouble He's my stay;*
> *He tells me every care on Him to roll;*
> *He's the Lily of the Valley,*
> *The Bright and Morning Star;*
> *He's the fairest of ten thousand to my soul.*[1]

MAGNIFY

In the science lab, magnification is used to study something. An object that's tiny will appear large under the magnification of a microscope. Something far away will appear to be near through a telescope. All these uses for magnification are for the purpose of examination. And it's all about appearances. The magnification doesn't change the substance—only the way it looks. So what does it mean to *magnify the Lord?*

Throughout the Old Testament, especially in the King James Version, the phrase appears many times. God tells Joshua that He will magnify him in the eyes of Israel just as He had done with Moses.

> This day will I begin to magnify thee in the sight of all Israel, that they may know that, as I was with Moses, so I will be with thee *(Joshua 3:7, KJV).*

Will Joshua's appearance change by the hand of God? Will he appear to be something he's not? Is he being or has he been examined?

Job asks a question of God:

> What is man, that thou shouldest magnify him? and that thou shouldest set thine heart upon him? *(Job 7:17, KJV).*

There is examination here just as there is in the science lab. It's stated that God will examine us every day. But does it in any way imply that this is about appearance and not about reality?

David wrote in a song:

> O magnify the LORD with me, and let us exalt his name together *(Psalm 34:3, KJV).*

Mary, a young virgin, finds out that she's pregnant with God's Son by a miracle of God's hand. Mary's first public statement about this is—

> My soul doth magnify the Lord *(Luke 1:46, KJV).*

I don't get the impression that David or Mary is trying to make God appear larger than He is or nearer than He is. I feel as though the magnification referred to in all accounts—and as it always relates to God—is how some Bible translations substitute the word *proclaim* for *magnify.*

Just as the word *glory* (see GLORY) implies, the verb *magnify* the Lord is to give an accurate accounting of who He really is. After all examination, the Lord is found to be worthy of the highest praise we can muster.

Dick and Mel Tunney wrote an exciting song of praise titled "O Magnify the Lord."

> *O magnify, O magnify the Lord with me,*
> *And let us exalt His name together!*
> *O magnify the Lord; O magnify the Lord;*
> *And may His name be lifted high forever!*[1]

Mel writes on her experience with the magnification of God:

Several years ago I had a close brush with blindness. Our family was heading to northern California for a week-long conference where Dick and I would lead worship and Chuck Swindoll was to be the speaker. I was at the mall picking up a few last-minute items for the trip and began to see spots before my eyes. By the time I got back home, the spots had enlarged, and by the time I was able to get to an ophthalmologist, I had lost the sight in my right eye.

I was rushed into surgery, and the doctors expressed that they hoped that my sight would be completely restored, but it wasn't something they could guarantee. The next several weeks of recovery were absolutely critical. I was to lie on my left side 24/7, sitting up only to eat or go to the restroom. I wasn't able to read, watch TV, or do anything that would require any eye movement.

To tell you the end of the story, my eye was completely healed. God, in His goodness and mercy to me, chose to give me back my sight.

It may sound funny to say this, but as my sight was limited in those weeks, the Lord became magnified in my life. John 3:30 says, "He must become greater, I must become less." His strength and power are made perfect in our weakness. And as we elevate and exalt Him, His glory is exhibited in fullest measure in our lives. Often our most difficult trials help us to see the greatness and fullness of our Lord.[2]

MAJESTY

I'm somewhat of a history geek. When a biography about America's second president, John Adams came out, I was fascinated. Most of the author's sources for the biography were from letters that John and his wife, Abigail, wrote to each other while he was away either serving in Congress or abroad as one of America's ambassadors to countries in Europe. I couldn't put the book down, for I was always anxious to find out what John and Abigail were up to.

One thing that impressed me was how fervently the fathers of our nation were fighting—both on the battlefield and in Congress—for the freedom we now enjoy. Those who had come to the New World were longing to get away from the despotic monarchs of Europe and to self-govern. Self-sovereignty was a new concept and rarely found anywhere else on the globe at that time.

However, with the gain of our freedom from monarchies, we lost the "majesty" that a king or a queen or the royal court commands.

Majesty denotes greatness, dignity, power, and splendor. But in a self-governing nation, we don't understand kingdom language such as this (see KINGDOM). I guess that's why we struggle with the sovereignty of God (see REIGN/SOVEREIGN).

Before the period of the kings in ancient Israel, majesty rose out of the role of the high priest. He was regal and revered and put in place by God. Then, when Jesus came along, He took the role of Eternal High Priest:

> The point of what we are saying is this: We do have such a high priest, who sat down at the right hand of the throne of the Majesty in heaven, and who serves in the sanctuary, the true tabernacle set up by the Lord, not by man *(Hebrews 8:1-2)*.

Pastor Jack Hayford, like many Americans, had not caught the concept of majesty either. He writes in his book *Worship His Majesty* of a personal experience that helped him embrace God's majestic qualities and prompted him to write a song that is sure to be sung for many, many years:

> For two weeks my wife, Anna, and I had been probing the corner of Scotland, Wales, and England in our tiny rental car. That summer the whole nation was enjoying a certain regal festivity as the silver anniversary of Elizabeth's coronation as

queen was being anticipated, and it was amid this prevailing air of rejoicing in royalty that we were introduced to England.

Occasionally I attempted to put into words the emotions I would feel as history spoke to me at every turn. Whether we were quietly sitting in a park or pushing our way through the crowds shopping at Harrods, an illusive sense of "the grand, the regal and the noble" caught my imagination and defied my efforts at definition. However, on a side trip we made in Oxfordshire, that definition came by surprise and included a lesson I hadn't expected and resulted in a song I hadn't sought.

Majesty

Majesty, worship His majesty,
Unto Jesus be all glory, honor, and praise.
Majesty, kingdom authority
Flow from His throne unto His own;
His anthem raise.[1]

As Queen Elizabeth's throne somehow dignifies every Englishman and makes multitudes of others partakers in a commonwealth of royal heritage, our ascended Savior sits enthroned and offers His regal resources to each of us.[2]

MORNING STAR

> *He's the Lily of the Valley,*
> *The Bright and Morning Star;*
> *He's the fairest of ten thousand to my soul.*[1]

The Bright and Morning Star mentioned in this old hymn is obviously referring to Jesus. Such reference to Jesus is found only in John's revelation, and it is Jesus' voice that John records here.

I, Jesus, have sent my angel to give you this testimony for the churches. I am the Root and the Offspring of David, and the bright Morning Star *(Revelation 22:16)*.

The metaphor is that Jesus, like the planet seen in the eastern sky around dawn, outshines all the other heavenly bodies. This may also be an indication that Jesus' coming marks the *dawning of a new day.*

Isaiah writes about a morning star in the Isaiah 14. However, this seems to be a narrative about the embodiment of Satan in the king of Babylon. Thus, the term *morning star* is a reference to the fleeting nature of the star appearing briefly but being overtaken by the sun.

The writer of the hymn "I Have Found a Friend in Jesus," I'm sure, could be speaking only of Christ, as He is exalted in John's revelation.

 NOEL

The first Noel the angels did say
Was to certain poor shepherds in fields as they lay—
In fields where they lay keeping their sheep
On a cold winter's night that was so deep.
Noel, Noel, Noel, Noel!
Born is the King of Israel![1]

You won't find the word *noel* in Scripture anywhere, but I felt it worthy of space in this book because we sing it at Christmastime each year. The word *noel* simply means "Christmas." It's from an old French word believed to be derived from the Latin word for the nativity, or the birth of Christ.

This carol may go back to the thirteenth century, but this hymn of unknown origin was officially printed in 1833 and has been a favorite in Christendom since.

Sometimes you'll see the word spelled *nowell,* which is the English derivative of the same word.

 OMNIPOTENT

The late great John W. Peterson wrote a song that I have heard and sung all my life: "It Took a Miracle."

> *My Father is omnipotent,*
> *And that you can't deny;*
> *A God of might and miracles—*
> *'Tis written in the sky.*[1]

I remember trying to sing this song early on with my dad and fumbling over the word *omnipotent*. Once I got the pronunciation right, I stayed in the dark about its meaning for many years after that.

Now I know. *Omni* means "all," and *potent* means "powerful," so *omnipotent* must mean "all-powerful."

You know we can't just leave it there. As this word describes God, there's much more to the concept. In the "Hallelujah Chorus" from Handel's *Messiah,* the word is almost as present as the hook "hallelujah" (see HALLELUJAH/ALLELUIA).

Handel cited Revelation 19 in the King James Version as one of his sources. John's vision of Jesus' return uses this word:

> And I heard as it were the voice of a great multitude, and as the voice of many waters, and as the voice of mighty thunderings, saying, Alleluia: for the Lord God omnipotent reigneth *(Revelation 19:6, KJV).*

The King James Version of the Bible is the only place I could find where this word is actually used in Scripture, and it's used only in this passage in Revelation. Most of the more modern translations of the Bible substitute *almighty* for *omnipotent* here (see EL SHADDAI/ALMIGHTY/MIGHTY).

The word still sounds somewhat lofty and undefined.

In God's covenant with David, the idea of an omnipotent, all-powerful God is softened with these words from the Almighty:

> I took you from the pasture and from following the flock to be ruler over my people Israel. I have been with you wherever you have gone, and I have cut off all your enemies from before you. Now I will make your name great, like the names of the greatest men of the earth *(2 Samuel 7:8-9).*

For an omnipotent Father to speak so sweetly to one of His children gives me another perspective on the idea of all-powerfulness. This attribute seems to be God's ability and willingness to do whatever He pleases.

Another word that's akin to *omnipotent* but not found much in songs is *omniscient.* It simply means all-knowing. It implies more than just knowledge. When attributed to God, *omniscience* indicates that He is also intimately informed and understanding of all our experiences. Picture this: an all-knowing Father who has all power to come to our aid, providing for us from His abundance. The psalmist says this of our *omnipotent* and *omniscient* God:

> He heals the brokenhearted and binds up their wounds. He determines the number of the stars and calls them each by name. Great is our Lord and mighty in power; his understanding has no limit *(Psalm 147: 3-5).*

Omnipresent isn't sung much either, but it finishes the trilogy of "omnis." The word means that God is everywhere all at once, not limited by finite things like time and space. The definition of the word may sound simple, but the concept is a mind-blower. Again to the Psalms:

> Where can I go from your Spirit? Where can I flee from your presence? If I go up to the heavens, you are there; if I make my bed in the depths, you are there. If I rise on the wings of the dawn, if I settle on the far side of the sea, even there your hand will guide me, your right hand will hold me fast *(Psalm 139:7-10).*

David looked through human eyes just as we do, but his faith and insight into God's presence in this lyric often takes my breath away. Psalm 139 as a whole is a beautiful lyric that I read often for hope and comfort.

 PEACE

Peace: it's probably humanity's greatest pursuit. It can also be Satan's greatest tool of deception—to whisper promises of peace into the ears of people looking for a quick path out of conflict.

The meaning of *peace,* in a spiritual sense, is far deeper than the thought that it is the opposite of conflict. The word and some of what it implies is worthy of space in this book, but I won't be able to fully explain it, because as Paul the apostle said in Philippians 4:7, it "passes all understanding."

As far as biblical history goes, the word *shalom* meant "peace" in Hebrew, and it was sometimes used as an antonym of fear. Gideon was visited by an angel with a message from God.

> The Lord said to him, Peace! Do not be afraid. You are not going to die *(Judges 6:23).*

And then it became a name for God or actually a place where God granted peace to Gideon. "Jehovah Shalom" is the Hebrew transliteration in the next verse.

> So Gideon built an altar to the Lord there and called it The Lord is Peace *(Judges 6:24).*

We also know that *shalom* was used as a greeting among the Hebrews. Apparently peace was something all wished for themselves and for others. Still, it was not until Isaiah came along that the word started to come into better focus. Isaiah, who wasn't known to write songs, wrote a lyric, and perhaps a tune, about it. It was a song of praise to God:

> You will keep in perfect peace him whose mind is steadfast, because he trusts in you *(Isaiah 26:3).*

Trust and a steadfast mind seemed to be prerequisites for a deeper peace—a perfect peace. But also remember that it was Isaiah who prophesied about the "Prince of Peace," who would come one day.

Even before His death and resurrection, Jesus talked about peace and then qualified it in His after-dinner speech to His disciples.

> Peace I leave with you; my peace I give you. I do not give to you as the world gives *(John 14:27).*

A new kind of peace? A super peace? Before, peace had been linked to a sense of well-being, fulfillment, lacking nothing essential. Was Jesus implying that this was a peace never before experienced? Later on in the speech, Jesus said,

I have told you these things, so that in me you may have peace. In this world you will have trouble. But take heart! I have overcome the world *(John 16:33)*.

Not long after this statement, Jesus went out to the garden to pray and was arrested there; and before another day had passed, He had suffered a violent execution. How could peace be found in such a situation?

Paul equates peace with being in harmony with God through a right standing through faith in His Son.

Since we have been justified through faith, we have peace with God through our Lord Jesus Christ, through whom we have gained access by faith into this grace in which we now stand *(Romans 5:1-2)*.

Though peace is mentioned in the New Testament as it relates to unity of the Church, this definition, "being in harmony with God," is what we find most in songs we sing today.

The songwriter who I feel captured the essence of peace is the late Horatio Spafford in his lyric to the hymn "It Is Well with My Soul."

> *When peace, like a river, attendeth my way,*
> *When sorrows like sea billows roll;*
> *Whatever my lot, Thou hast taught me to say,*
> *It is well, it is well with my soul.*[1]

These words become even more powerful when one knows the story behind them.

Spafford was a successful lawyer in Chicago in the mid-1800s. During the great Chicago fire of 1871, Spafford lost a lot of property. The stress of the loss prompted Horatio and his family to take a vacation in Europe. On the scheduled departure date in November 1873, Horatio was detained with business matters, but he sent his wife and four daughters ahead to sail the ocean on the *S. S. Ville du Havre.* En route, the ship collided with an English vessel and sank in a matter of minutes. Mrs. Spafford survived, but all four girls were lost at sea.

Spafford boarded another ship immediately to meet his despondent wife in England. As the ship approached the place where the S. S. Ville du Havre had sunk, Horatio asked the captain to stop while he wrote the lyrics to his now-beloved song. The chorus echoes:

> *It is well with my soul,*
> *It is well, it is well with my soul.*

This is true peace—not the peace the world gives but peace that passes human understanding. It is enduring harmony with God in the middle of life's tragedy and heartache.

 RANSOM

Our sign said "Lost! Reward!"

Our dog had run away—again—and this time he hadn't returned right away. All the neighbors knew that our Yorkie was prone to wander, so they knew to be on the lookout, but by that evening still no one had seen him.

We got desperate the next day and put up signs in a nearby grocery store. We were eager to pay whatever sum we could to get him back. We were pretty sure that he hadn't been stolen, but even if he had been kidnapped, we thought he was worth whatever it took for his safe return.

The word *ransom* is used in many worship songs and hymns, and while it doesn't apply directly to my dog story, it does imply payment for the release of a prisoner or hostage—a trade.

In a biblical context the *ransom* literally means the price paid to redeem something, which is in pledge or in pawn, or the purchase price paid or received for the liberation of a slave.

Since slavery doesn't exist in most cultures in the world today, that definition is a little puzzling. Let's go back to its original use for clarity.

In the Old Testament there was a slave, an owner, and a price that was paid for the slave's freedom. The price was whatever the owner set it to be.

Slavery was still in practice in New Testament times, so the word still had meaning, but it went from something concrete to abstract when Jesus referred to himself in Matthew 20:28—

> The Son of Man did not come to be served, but to serve, and to give his life as a ransom for many.

We know now that the price for our freedom from an eternity of separation from God was Jesus' physical life. Paul told the Corinthians,

> God made him who had no sin to be sin for us, so that in him we might become the righteousness of God *(2 Corinthians 5:21).*

God made Jesus, who knew no sin himself, to become sin so we could be made right in His eyes (see RIGHTEOUSNESS)—a trade, His Son's life for our freedom. And furthermore, according to Paul's letter, Jesus didn't just pay our ransom—He *was* our ransom.

So to whom was our ransom paid?

Nowhere in the New Testament are there any words suggesting to whom that price was paid. I don't think it could have been paid to God, because He loved the world and was not holding it hostage. It probably wasn't to be paid to the devil, for that would put the devil in a deal-making posture with God. All we know is that it cost the life and death of Christ to liberate humanity from the past, the present, and the future power of sin. In the hymn "Praise, My Soul, the King of Heaven" the lyricist almost defines the word *ransom* with the words that follow it.

> *Praise, my soul, the King of heaven,*
> *To His feet thy tribute bring;*
> *Ransomed, healed, restored, forgiven,*
> *Evermore His praises sing.*
> *Alleluia! Alleluia!*
> *Praise the everlasting King!*[1]

The end of my lost-dog story:

The phone rang, and a distant neighbor said she had seen our sign in a grocery store window. She had found our dog a couple of days before and was keeping him safe until she could locate the owner. When we went to get him, he was freshly shampooed and eating out of a china dish. (I thought he actually rolled his eyes when we walked in.) His new friend wouldn't take a reward, so there was no ransom needed in this case.

I would like to say that this was the dog's last self-guided journey, but it wasn't. His instinct for freedom was strong, and he tested our nerves and patience until the day he died.

 REDEEM / REDEEMER

I grew up in the days of S & H Green Stamps.

At the checkout line at the store, depending on the amount of
the purchase, we were given a perforated sheet of green stamps,
each one worth a certain amount of buying power. After we had
collected a good number of stamps, my sister and I would lick them
on the sticky side and press them into a book. We had a catalog
with pictures of all kinds of wonderful items we could buy with our
stamps: toys, household items, and so forth, each with a picture of
the item and the number of books of stamps required to purchase it.
As soon as we had enough stamp books, we went to a redemption
center and traded them in for the items we had dreamed about.

The idea of trading in something for something else is the basic definition of the word *redeem.* The act of redemption is closely related to the definition for *ransom* (see RANSOM), which means the price paid out for something.

At first, historically, the term *redeem* was purely a legal term used in commercial trade—a simple transaction in which one good was traded for another. But in Exodus 21:29-30 it was expanded to include humans or other living things:

> If, however, the bull has had the habit of goring and the owner has been warned but has not kept it penned up and it kills a man or woman, the bull must be stoned and the owner also must be put to death. However, if payment is demanded of him, he may redeem his life by paying whatever is demanded.

The Hebrew word *ga'al* translated as *redeem* and included an act of obligation—or sometimes mercy—related to a next-of-kin who had lost rights to family property for one reason or another. Ruth, a young widow, went to a stranger, Boaz, who happened to be a distant relative of her dead husband. Boaz became her kinsman-redeemer who purchased her late husband's land to keep it from falling into unrelated hands. Of course, the story includes Ruth's eventual marriage to Boaz that produced a son who in a few more generations produced King David—and ultimately Jesus.

Finally, however, the idea of redemption was transferred to Jesus' blood. He was the substitute sacrifice to buy us out of bondage from the penalty of breaking the law, from certain acts of sin itself, and the guilt that accompanies both.

> Christ redeemed us from the curse of the law by becoming a curse for us, for it is written: "Cursed is everyone who is hung on a tree" (Galatians 3:13).

Later in Galatians Paul writes,

> When the time had fully come, God sent his Son, born of a woman, born under law, to redeem those under law, that we might receive the full rights of sons (Galatians 4:4-5).

So the ransom, the payment from our slavery to all that's evil, implies a release as well—to freedom, to sonship, and to eternal life. We're even released—*redeemed*—from a life that is without meaning to one that is meaningful. Peter wrote,

> You know that it was not with perishable things such as silver or gold that you were redeemed from the empty way of life handed down to you from your forefathers (1 Peter 1:18).

Eric Wyse and Dawn Rodgers Wyse wrote a beautiful song, "Wonderful, Merciful, Savior."

> *Wonderful, merciful, Savior,*
> *Precious Redeemer and Friend;*
> *Who would have thought that a Lamb*
> *Could rescue the souls of men?*
> *O You rescue the souls of men.*[1]

Dawn gives personal insight into the word *Redeemer.*

Redeemer: my favorite name for Jesus. It humbles me, centers me, reminds me that I need something—need Someone. I need my worthlessness to be exchanged for worthiness. Only Jesus can do that for me. Only He can reach into the dark despair of emptiness and fill it with joy and peace and hope. Precious Redeemer and Friend.[2]

 REIGN / SOVEREIGN

As I write this, there are only four, if you count Vatican City as a sovereign state, absolute monarchies left on earth. Yes, there are still single heads of state who exercise ultimate power to rule the citizens of their countries without opposition or higher bodies of governing law. Popular sovereignties exist elsewhere in the world, but these monarchs do not rule alone or without the basic consent of the governed.

So by definition, a true sovereign or absolute ruler over a people is quite rare today. Maybe that's why it's hard for us to see God in this role as *Absolute Sovereign*—one who possesses and executes supreme authority and power over His charges.

Moses understood God's reign. He saw even the powers of natural law succumb to the overwhelming power of God's deliberate hand when the Red Sea parted, allowing Moses and his charges to escape the grasp of Egypt's sovereignty. Moses and his sister wrote a song about it. Here's part of the lyric.

The Lord will reign for ever and ever *(Exodus 15:18)*.

King David of old seemed to have no problem with God's reign either. He recognized the limits of his own powers when he acknowledged God as his Supreme Authority and Provider.

Listen to my cry for help, my King and my God, for to you I pray *(Psalm 5:2)*.

So why is it so hard for us to define and embrace the idea of God's absolute power over us now? The story of Eden suggests that we might have been initially wired that way. Along with healthy curiosity and a little whimsy, we apparently got a thirst for power. Eve's believing and then acting upon the serpent's lies about the divine hierarchy somehow brought with it doubt about God being in control. Not only that, but we also started doubting that He was looking out for our best interests. Has our itch to rule ourselves strengthened through the centuries? Is that something we can fix?

Even if we can't see or fix our need to rule or govern ourselves, it doesn't change the fact that God still possesses absolute power. We can doubt it and fight it, but it will not alter His place in the hierarchy as Absolute Ruler.

The kingdom of the world has become the kingdom of our Lord and of his Christ, and he will reign for ever and ever *(Revelation 11:15).*

Charles Wesley, who wrote the lyrics to the great majestic hymn "Rejoice, the Lord Is King," embraced the idea of God's sovereignty:

> *Rejoice, the Lord is King:*
> *Your Lord and King adore!*
> *Rejoice, give thanks, and sing,*
> *And triumph evermore.*
> *Lift up your heart;*
> *Lift up your voice!*
> *Rejoice; again I say: rejoice!*
>
> *Jesus, the Savior, reigns,*
> *The God of truth and love.*
> *When He had purged our stains,*
> *He took His seat above.*
> *Lift up your heart;*
> *Lift up your voice!*
> *Rejoice; again I say: rejoice!*
>
> *His kingdom cannot fail,*
> *He rules o'er earth and heaven;*
> *The keys of death and hell*
> *Are to our Jesus given.*
> *Lift up your heart;*

Lift up your voice!
Rejoice; again I say: rejoice![1]

Even if you don't understand how the kingdom of God works, it's at least good to know the wide range of truths stated in that hymn (see KINGDOM). First, He is King; Jesus took our sins and then took His seat in heaven. His kingdom never fails. It includes earth and heaven. Finally, Jesus holds the keys to death and hell. What a relief! Somebody else is in charge, and I don't have to be.

 REJOICE

One of my happiest days is the day I found out I was pregnant with our first child. We had some reason to fear that we would never have children at all, so when the doctor gave us news, you can say I rejoiced. I don't remember saying the word *rejoice,* but it's safe to say that I most certainly rejoiced in the announcement of my pregnancy to others. By the way, I was just as ecstatic when I found out I was pregnant the second time.

Rejoice is an action that comes out of a heart full of gratitude. It implies "exuberance" as in the excitement of a sports fan when his or her team scores. It even means "to boast," which follows the sports fan comparison.

David was rejoicing verbally, boasting about the Lord in Psalm 16:8-9.

I have set the LORD always before me. Because he is at my right hand, I will not be shaken. Therefore my heart is glad and my tongue rejoices.

In two of Jesus' lost-and-found parables (Luke 15:6, 9), the shepherd who had lost a sheep and the woman who had lost a coin invited others to rejoice with them when they finally found what they were looking for. Rejoicing goes beyond boasting and exuberance to cheerleading and party planning. The parable implies that there was an all-out party to celebrate the finds.

In Paul's letter to the Philippians, there's a party atmosphere because of the faith that the church at Philippi was experiencing.

> Even if I am being poured out like a drink offering on the sacrifice and service coming from your faith, I am glad and rejoice with all of you. So you too should be glad and rejoice with me *(Philippians 2:17-18)*.

Even though Paul was suffering physically, he was able to celebrate with his friends. So it's clear that rejoicing can take place even when one is experiencing hardship. How can that be?

Paul answers that question in his letter to the Roman Christians.

> Since we have been justified through faith, we have peace with God through our Lord Jesus Christ, through whom we have gained access by faith into this grace in which we now stand. And we rejoice in the hope of the glory of God *(Romans 5:1-2)*.

There's so much in those two verses to rejoice about! Peace with God, access to Him, His grace to stand on, the hope of His glory! (See PEACE, GRACE, HOPE, GLORY).

There's reference in Scripture to other parts of God's creation, besides humanity, having the ability to rejoice. The psalmist more than implies this:

> Let the heavens rejoice, let the earth be glad; let the sea resound, and all that is in it; let the fields be jubilant, and everything in them. Then all the trees of the forest will sing for joy; they will sing before the Lord *(Psalm 96:11-13).*

Gary Sadler and Paul Baloche wrote a great praise song about the rejoicing of creation. The verse in the song "Rise Up and Praise Him" was taken from Psalm 96.

> *Let the heavens rejoice,*
> *Let the earth be glad,*
> *Let the people of God,*
> *Sing His praise*
> *All over the land.*
> *Everyone in the valley,*
> *Come and lift your voice.*
> *All those on the mountaintop,*
> *Be glad and shout for joy.*[1]

RIGHTEOUS / RIGHTEOUSNESS

Here's some advice we received before moving into a new house: "If you want your marriage to remain strong, never hang wallpaper together." We did not heed the advice, but our marriage survived.

Some of the lessons we learned from the experience, though, are quite profound. First—which is not so profound—is that no room is perfect. Not all drywall is completely smooth, and corners are not always at absolute right angles. Second, to get wallpaper to hang straight, you use the natural pull of gravity. You must hang a plumb line from the ceiling. The string hanging between the ceiling and the weight at the bottom will give you a perfect perpendicular line to guide you as you hang the first piece of paper. That's the profound part. Start with a something that's perfect and true.

If righteousness has an earthly comparison, maybe the plumb line lesson is it.

Righteousness has sometimes been translated—when it comes to God—as being "just." But God's righteousness seems to refer to more than that, like His moral excellence, His purity, His consistency in dealing with His people. That part is understandable. Being righteous means perfection when attributed to Almighty God.

However, in Psalm 7 David uses the word *righteous* to describe both God and humanity.

> O righteous God, who searches minds and hearts, bring to an end the violence of the wicked and make the righteous secure *(Psalm 7:9)*.

If God is "true" and "perfect," how can flawed humanity be as well?

From the beginning, humanity's righteousness has been given to them by God. Abram was promised a son who would be the beginning of a great nation, and God said this about that:

> He [God] took him [Abram] outside and said, "Look up at the heavens and count the stars—if indeed you can count them." Then he said to him, "So shall your offspring be." Abram believed the Lord, and he credited it to him as righteousness *(Genesis 15:5-6)*.

If the plumb line illustration holds, then our righteousness—our right-ness—would come from an anchor to God, a standard that only He can set and commute to others. But it must also involve faith.

In New Testament language our righteousness seems to come through faith in Christ.

2 Corinthians 5:21 states,
> God made him who had no sin to be sin for us, so that in him we might become the righteousness of God.

In other words, we can be "plumbed, squared with God, because Jesus became our sin, which was then crucified" (see CROSS and see ATONEMENT).

Many songs tell of God's righteousness. "How Firm a Foundation," "Joy to the World." Not as many songs speak of our righteousness. However, Sandra Corbett-Wood's "I Worship You, Almighty God," speaks of giving praise to God for giving right-ness with Him.

> *I worship You, Almighty God;*
> *There is none like You.*
> *I worship You, O Prince of Peace;*
> *That is what I want to do.*
> *I give You praise,*
> *For You are my righteousness.*
> *I worship You, Almighty God;*
> *There is none like You.*[1]

ROCK

Everybody knows what a rock is. But why is God sometimes compared to a rock in Scripture, and why do we use this comparison in our hymns and worship songs?

The metaphor goes at least as far back as the patriarch Jacob. In Jacob's blessing to his twelve sons (who would become the twelve tribes of Israel), he calls God "the Rock." In his blessing to Joseph, Jacob says of his favorite son,

> His bow remained steady, his strong arms stayed limber, because of the hand of the Mighty One of Jacob, because of the Shepherd, the Rock of Israel *(Genesis 49:24).*

In those days particularly, the rocky cliffs of the Middle East represented places of protection, hiding places as in a crevice, a cleft, or a cave. These places for King David were points of refuge when he was running and hiding from his enemies. For Elijah the prophet, a rocky crevice was a place where he went to talk to God in private and where God met with him and spoke with him in a special way. The same with Moses. Moses went up into the rocky cliffs to receive the law from God. So comparing God to a rock often meant a place of refuge, protection, and strength.

But Isaiah also received a word from the Lord that scholars believe is a word of prophecy about a coming Messiah:

> See, I lay a stone in Zion, a tested stone, a precious cornerstone for a sure foundation; the one who trusts will never be dismayed *(Isaiah 28:16)*.

Here, still, the theme of the Rock being a place of strength is used but probably was starting to include the coming Savior (see SAVIOR and see ZION).

As time went on, the metaphor of the rock had evolved enough that Jesus himself used it to describe "a secure place" that could hold the weight of a house, comparing it, as Isaiah had introduced, with a firm foundation.

> Everyone who hears these words of mine and puts them into practice is like a wise man who built his house on the rock *(Matthew 7:24)*.

Though the association to God or Jesus in this illustration isn't really obvious, it has been interpreted to mean that Jesus was making a statement about himself and His kingdom (see KINGDOM).

Think about this reference when you sing "The Solid Rock."

> *My hope is built on nothing less*
> *Than Jesus' blood and righteousness;*
> *I dare not trust the sweetest frame,*
> *But wholly lean on Jesus' name.*

> *On Christ, the solid Rock, I stand;*
> *All other ground is sinking sand,*
> *All other ground is sinking sand.*[1]

Later in Scripture Paul reaches back into history to a time when the children of Israel were wandering in the wilderness and were thirsty. Moses struck a rock, and water came forth. Paul's reference to that story in 1 Corinthians 10:3-4 contrasts Christ with the water-giving rock.

> They all ate the same spiritual food and drank the same spiritual drink; for they drank from the spiritual rock that accompanied them, and that rock was Christ.

So when you sing about the *Rock,* think of God as a place of safety, a place of strength, a reliable building site, and a life-giving source.

The old hymn "Rock of Ages" was written to bring comfort to a grieving heart. Often sung at funerals, the first verse says,

> Rock of Ages, cleft for me,
> Let me hide myself in Thee;
> Let the water and the blood,
> From Thy wounded side which flowed,
> Be of sin the double cure,
> Save from wrath and make me pure.[2]

SABAOTH (OR SABBAOTH)

Sabaoth is not a "singing" word exactly and therefore not used often in modern hymns and songs, but I include it in this book because of its prominence in a great hymn of our faith. With words and music written around 1529 or so, the great reformer Martin Luther wrote this:

> *Did we in our own strength confide,*
> *Our striving would be losing;*
> *Were not the right Man on our side,*
> *The Man of God's own choosing.*
> *Dost ask who that may be?*
> *Christ Jesus it is He,*
> *Lord Sabaoth His name.*
> *From age to age the same*
> *And He must win the battle.*[1]

The song's inspiration obviously came from Psalm 46:7:

The LORD Almighty is with us; the God of Jacob is our fortress.

But where did the word *Sabaoth* come from?

Because the word looks like the word *Sabbath,* some people think that it refers to God as He commands that we take a day of the week for worship and rest. But in its translation—translated literally "Lord of Hosts"—it doesn't appear to refer to the Sabbath at all.

The word seems to have originated at a place of worship, however, called Shiloh, in the days of the priest Samuel. Shiloh had become a place where worshipers gathered to make offerings and to receive something, a word or blessings, from the Lord through the priests. It was about thirty miles north of Jerusalem and was the home at that time of the tabernacle in ancient Israel (see TABERNACLE/ TEMPLE).

This is where the word *Sabaoth* enters Scripture. In the first chapter of 1 Samuel the name "LORD of hosts" is written in the narrative; however, it seems to have been spoken first by a young childless woman named Hannah.

And she vowed a vow, and said, O LORD of hosts, if thou wilt indeed look on the affliction of thine handmaid, and remember me, and not forget thine handmaid, but wilt give unto thine handmaid a man child, then I will give him unto the LORD all the days of his life *(1 Samuel 1:11, KJV).*

Most scholars believe that *Sabaoth* and *Lord of Hosts* are used synonymously in the Bible, and most agree that they refer to God's command of the armies of angels who surround His throne, since the word *host* often implies "army." It is also said that the name may refer to God's command over all things. That's why some translations of the Bible use Lord Almighty (see ALMIGHTY/EL SHADDAI/MIGHTY) in this place.

Even though Samuel and Hannah first coined the phrase *Lord of hosts,* the name for God seemed to stick, for it is carried on through the days of King David and the prophets Elijah, Isaiah, and Jeremiah. In the New Testament, Paul and James each quote from the prophets, restating the name *Sabaoth* to the young Church. In the Old Testament, at least, the word *Sabaoth* seemed to be a cry for help for those who had found that their own resources are inadequate in the middle of a struggle.

Sabaoth. Perhaps we should bring the word back to lyrics today. Well, maybe not, but its synonym "Lord of Hosts" should at least be a cry on our lips, especially when we discover that we've exhausted all of own strength in our life struggles.

SAVIOR / SALVATION

Ah, the old hymns about salvation! One of my favorites is "Face to Face with Christ, My Savior"

> Face to Face with Christ, My Savior,
> Face to face—what will it be
> When with rapture I behold Him,
> Jesus Christ, who died for me?[1]

It speaks of Jesus the Savior, but as many other songs of salvation, it refers to Him only in terms of heaven—seeing Him in the "by and by." So does the Savior do His saving only after we die? And what are we saved from anyway?

Well, the word *Savior,* as it relates to Jesus, has been defined as rescuer or deliverer of humanity from the penalty and power of sin.

At first, in the Old Testament the salvation of God didn't necessarily link to the forgiveness of sins. It mostly referred to deliverance from slavery, oppression, or ungodly enemies.

David's Song of Praise recorded in 2 Samuel 22:2-3 suggests that salvation was being viewed as physical:

The LORD is my rock, my fortress and my deliverer; my God is my rock, in whom I take refuge, my shield and the horn of my salvation. He is my stronghold, my refuge and my savior—from violent men you save me.

God even says of himself that He was the Savior from physical bondage:

I am the LORD your God, who brought you out of Egypt. You shall acknowledge no God but me, no Savior except me (Hosea 13:4).

However, beginning with Isaiah 6, the idea of salvation started to take on an eternal meaning. God apparently was preparing His people for something more than deliverance from enemies of this life and started pointing them to the coming Messiah. In Isaiah 51:6 God declares,

My salvation will last forever, my righteousness will never fail.

The first clue that Jesus would be a Savior like no other was in an angel's appearance to Jesus' stepfather, Joseph, before the Child was born:

Joseph son of David, do not be afraid to take Mary home as your wife, because what is conceived in her is from the Holy Spirit. She will give birth to a son, and you are to give him the name Jesus, because he will save his people from their sins *(Matthew 1:20-21)*.

This was a pretty radical thought to a people who were looking for a warrior like King David, not a spiritual kingdom (see KINGDOM).

In a hillside revelation from an angel, the newborn Jesus was called Savior for the first time.

Unto you is born this day in the city of David a Savior, which is Christ the Lord *(Luke 2:11, KJV)*.

As years went by and Jesus grew into His earthly ministry, some were still thinking that He would bring salvation from the oppression of the Romans. Others saw Him as the Deliverer from disease. Disease had a stronghold on this generation, and since little was known of the causes and cures of most maladies, the Savior gave them a welcome cure.

But when Jesus went to the Cross, everything changed. He had started preparing the people for what was to come and had said of himself in Mark 10:45,

Even the Son of Man did not come to be served, but to serve, and to give his life as a ransom for many (see RANSOM).

For God so loved the world, that He gave His only begotten

Son; that whosoever believeth in Him should not perish, but have everlasting life *(John 3:16, KJV)*.

So His salvation wasn't just from temporal enemies but from eternal separation from God. So what was then the extent of His saving power?

Romans 8:31-35, 37 seems to cover salvation from everything else on this side of heaven, making Christ's salvation comprehensive.

> If God is for us, who can be against us? He who did not spare his own Son, but gave him up for us all—how will he not also, along with him, graciously give us all things? Who will bring any charge against those whom God has chosen? It is God who justifies. Who is he that condemns? Christ Jesus, who died— more than that, who was raised to life—is at the right hand of God and is also interceding for us. Who shall separate us from the love of Christ? Shall trouble or hardship or persecution or famine or nakedness or danger or sword? *(Romans 8:31-35)*.

Saved from death? Yes. Saved from earthly woes, like injustice, persecution, want? Yes.

> In all these things we are more than conquerors through him who loved us *(Romans 8:37)*.

I love the chorus to "There Is a Savior," by Greg Nelson, Bob Farrell, and Sandi Patti. In that one chorus the Savior's attributes and eternal guidance are a soothing thought.

> *There is a Savior,*
> *What joys express!*
> *His eyes are mercy,*
> *His word is rest.*
> *For each tomorrow,*
> *For yesterday,*
> *There is a Savior*
> *Who lights our way.*[2]

Bob Farrell adds, "The Savior I write about has always been One who gives comfort in our distress, light in our confusion, mercy in our failures, peace in our unrest—a personal Savior in every aspect and situation in our lives."[3]

TABERNACLE / TEMPLE

I remember the days of tent revivals. As a child, I considered it a bit of a spectacle, an event I kind of enjoyed. I remember wondering, *Why are we having church outside with the heat, the bugs, and the humidity when there are perfectly good buildings all around where we can be more comfortable?*

The temporary church house—a tent of meeting—is an old concept. Even as far back as Moses, the Tabernacle, which was a temporary building for the purpose of meeting with God, was sanctioned. Shortly after the Ten Commandments were given through Moses, God wanted His people to construct such a place.

> Have them make a sanctuary for me, and I will dwell among them. Make this tabernacle and all its furnishings exactly like the pattern I will show you *(Exodus 25:8-9)*.

At that time, the Israelites were a nomadic people who couldn't build a permanent structure they would eventually have to abandon. But that was no excuse. The ark of the covenant needed a place to be sheltered, and the priests also needed a location to accept the sacrifices of the people.

God through Moses dictated everything about the Tabernacle, from the furniture to the decorations to the robes worn by the priests. Read all about it in Exodus 25-28. It's pretty amazing.

The Tabernacle was the movable dwelling place of God, His sanctuary.

The song "God of Wonders" speaks of the heavens themselves being God's tabernacle. What a beautiful picture of God's presence!

> Lord of all creation,
> Of water, earth, and sky,
> The heavens are Your tabernacle;
> Glory to the Lord on high.[1]

Here is an aside about the song "God of Wonders," written by Marc Byrd and Steve Hindalong: It was requested by astronaut Commander Rick Husband to be played on the Space Shuttle Columbia as his wake-up call. On February 1, 2003, Rick and his crew were killed as the shuttle disintegrated while reentering the atmosphere.

The temporary meeting place, the *Tabernacle,* was finally replaced during the reign of King David's son, Solomon. And oh, what a place that was! Read about that in 1 Kings 5 and 6.

As with the Tabernacle, the Temple was known as "the house of God." It was His dwelling place. That place went from a fixed dwelling that housed the presence of God in the Old Testament to the housing of God's Spirit in the lives of believers after Pentecost. And yet God still lives in the heavenly realm, too.

The old call to worship "The Lord Is in His Holy Temple" got its text from Habakkuk 2:20.

> *The Lord is in His holy temple,*
> *The Lord is in His holy temple;*
> *Let all the earth keep silence,*
> *Let all the earth keep silence before Him,*
> *Keep silence, keep silence before Him.*[2]

Habakkuk ended one of his laments with this similar statement:

> The LORD is in his holy temple; let all the earth be silent before him.

This was a reminder then as it is today, that God is alive and rules over all the nations from His throne in heaven. But in New Testament terms it reassures us that God still lives here among us in the hearts of His people.

WORSHIP

Worship is a hot topic.

The mere mention of it will bring up lots of opinions, questions, and perhaps even controversy. Worship has been studied and analyzed for centuries, but no more than in the past decade. Worship songs have become a genre within the genre of Christian music, and the debates about authenticity of worship abound. Worship has become somewhat of a science, but also it has perhaps become an art form—at least as defined in the corporate sense.

And speaking of the corporate sense, doesn't the word *worship* usually invoke a picture of a gathering of believers on a Sunday morning? Out of this reference alone, schools and seminars have been established to teach us about worship. There are volumes of books and articles and magazines on the topic.

How can we know what worship is, but, more important, how do we do it as God intended? In this chapter we will not answer all the questions. We probably won't even scratch the surface, but hopefully we'll get a better picture of what we're singing about.

Historically, corporate worship was mandated under Moses' leadership of the Israelites. Starting in the middle chapters of the Book of Exodus, instructions were sent down from God about the preparations of a place for all to meet and worship. Before that, the patriarchs had made sacrifices and built altars whenever and wherever they wanted to worship God. There were strict rules about the order of worship, who could lead worship, and specifically what things could be done during the times of worship. It always involved *acts,* however, done in reverence to God.

Years later, the "new covenant" people gathered, not just on the Sabbath or the Lord's Day, to maintain this tradition. New Testament corporate worship included preaching, the reading of scripture, prayer, singing, baptism, the Lord's Supper, and the giving of monetary offerings. Sounds familiar, doesn't it?

Since *worship* is both a noun and a verb, it probably has something to do with both attitude and action. Dictionary definitions include, as a verb, "to revere, to pay homage to, to express feelings of awe, to act piously toward." And as a noun, it's a "rite or service through which people show their adoration and devotion to God."

Since worship and music have become so closely tied together, it really would serve us well to stop here and see it through the eyes of some worship leaders.

Rick Muchow, the Pastor of Worship at Saddleback Church in southern California, not only leads many corporate worship services every week but has also written a book titled *The Worship Answer Book: More than a Music Experience.* Here Rick points out that music itself isn't necessarily worship but can be the language of worship— that it can be one way of expressing our love for God.

Matt Redman's song "Heart of Worship" came out of an experience in his home church in England.

A few years back in our church, we realized some of the things we thought were helping us in our worship were actually hindering us. They were throwing us off the scent of what it means to really worship.

Mike, the pastor, decided on a pretty drastic course of action: we'd strip everything away for a season, just to see where our hearts were. So the very next Sunday when we turned up at church, there was no sound system to be seen and no band to lead us.

If I'm honest, at first I was pretty offended by the whole thing. The worship was my job! But as God softened my heart, I started to see His wisdom all over these actions.

After a while, the worship band and the sound system reappeared, but now it was different. The songs of our hearts had caught up with the songs of our lips.[1]

Out of this experience Matt wrote this song:

> When the music fades,
> All is stripped away,
> And I simply come;
> Longing just to bring something that's of worth
> That will bless Your heart.
>
> I'll bring You more than a song,
> For a song in itself
> Is not what You have required.
> You search much deeper within
> Through the way things appear;
> You're looking into my heart.
>
> I'm coming back to the heart of worship,
> And it's all about You,
> All about You, Jesus.
> I'm sorry, Lord, for the thing I've made it,
> When it's all about You,
> All about You, Jesus.[2]

I also like what Chris Tomlin, one of the writers of the popular song "Made to Worship," says about worship. This hits more on an individual, personal worship level.

Worship isn't really a churchy word. Everyone worships something. And what you worship is whatever you place the highest value on. It's what you order your choices by, what you surrender your will to. So while most of us say, "Hey—you won't find any stone idols at my house!" we don't really own up to what we do worship.[3]

Paul the apostle seemed to think this defines worship, too. In his letter to the Roman Christians he makes a pretty bold statement:

I urge you, brothers, in view of God's mercy, to offer your bodies as living sacrifices, holy and pleasing to God-this is your spiritual act of worship *(Romans 12:1).*

I think Paul is addressing the attitude that's most certainly included in the act of worship and in the attitude of worship. Surrender. Sacrifice. Pleasing. Holiness (see HOLY). All of these should be present in both our personal worship and when we gather with others to worship.

Do these insights make the word *worship* any easier to understand? I don't know if they do. Are there still more questions about worship? I hope so. Perhaps questions will remain and create a thirst that will make us all want to seek a closer worship relationship with God.

ZION / MOUNT ZION

At least as far back as when David reigned as Israel's king, the capital city of Israel was Jerusalem, which sat on a place called *Mount Zion.* Jerusalem and the surrounding area were often referred to simply as *Zion.* After the city of Jerusalem, which was thought to be unconquerable, fell into enemy hands many times, the term *Zion* began to take on a different meaning. Biblical writers began to use the word to symbolize the dwelling place of God (see TABERNACLE/TEMPLE).

In Psalm 48:1-2 the writer called the mountain "holy":

Great is the LORD, and most worthy of praise, in the city of our God, his holy mountain. It is beautiful in its loftiness, the joy of the whole earth. Like the utmost heights of Zaphon is Mount Zion, the city of the Great King.

Even later, *Zion* began to refer to the eternal City of God, the New Jerusalem, and the dwelling place to which all believers will eventually go—heaven.

> You have come to Mount Zion, to the heavenly Jerusalem, the city of the living God. You have come to thousands upon thousands of angels in joyful assembly, to the church of the firstborn, whose names are written in heaven. You have come to God, the judge of all men, to the spirits of righteous men made perfect, to Jesus the mediator of a new covenant *(Hebrews 12:22-24).*

The chorus to the hymn "We're Marching to Zion" later added to the original lyric by music composer Robert Lowry, definitely refers to heaven and celebrates the time when all believers will enter the New Jerusalem (see JERUSALEM/NEW JERUSALEM).

> *We're marching to Zion,*
> *Beautiful, beautiful Zion;*
> *We're marching upward to Zion,*
> *The beautiful city of God.*[1]

ABBA

1. stevenfryministries.com. Steve Fry serves as senior past of The Gate, a church in Franklin, Tennessee. He is also the president of Messenger Fellowship. As a pastor, author, composer, and recording artist, Steve blends worship and scriptural teaching in a way that's relevant and revelatory. Steve received his master's degree in theology from Syndney College of Divinity. He has served as a board member of many local and national ministries and in 2007 became president for the International Worship institute (worshipinstitute.com).

2. Steve Fry, "Abba Father," © 1979 Birdwing Music/BMG Songs, Inc.

3. Submitted for this book by Steve Fry. Used with permission.

ADONAI / LORD

1. Paul Baloche, "Praise Adonai," © 1999 Integrity's Hosanna! Music. Used by permission.

2. Paul Baloche, leadworship.com. Used by permission.

ALLELUIA / HALLELUJAH

1. Steve Green began his singing ministry with the group Truth and later with the Gaithers. He has four Grammy nominations, thirteen number-one songs, and seven Dove Awards. So far Steve has twenty-nine recordings, including children's project and Spanish-language albums. He has sold more than three million albums worldwide. Steve has been married to Marijean for more than thirty years, and they have two children and one grandchild. stevegreenministries.org

2. Steve Green, "Antiphonal Praise," © 1990 Birdwing Music (a div. of EMI Christian Music Publishing). Used by permission.

3. Written for this book by Steve Green. Used with permission.

ALPHA AND OMEGA

1. Charles Wesley and John Zundel, "Love Divine, All Loves Excelling" 1747, public domain.

AMEN

1. Matt Redman, mattredman.com

2. Joachim Neander and Stralsund Gesangbuch, "Praise to the Lord, the Almighty," 1680, public domain.

ANCIENT OF DAYS

1. Robert Grant, Johann Michael Haydn, "O Worship the King," 1833, public domain.

2. Chance Scoggins is a session vocalist, songwriter, and Dove Award-winning producer. His list of production and arranging credits include Mandisa, Matthew West, Avalon, Point of Grace, Don Moen, Women of Faith, Michael W. Smith, Amy Grant, and many others. He traveled with Bible teacher Beth Moore as a part of her worship team for ten years and recently collaborated with her on *An Invitation to Freedom,* which he considers his most important work to day.

3. Chance Scoggins, Travis Cottrell, "Now and Forevermore," © 1998, Van Ness Press, Inc. (Admin. by LifeWay Christian Resources, First Hand Revelation Music; Chance-A-Lot Music, Inc.). Used by permission.

4. Written for this book by Chance Scoggins. Used with permission.

ATONEMENT
1. Fanny Crosby, William Doane, "To God Be the Glory," 1875, public domain.

BALM IN GILEAD
1. Traditional Spiritual, "Balm in Gilead," public domain.

BANNER
1. Daniel Webster Whittle, James McGranahan, "The Banner of the Cross," 1885, public domain.
2. Christ Tomlin, Jesse Reeves, "Not to Us," ©2001, worshiptogether. com songs (Admin. by EMI Christian Music Publishing) sixsteps Music (Admin. by EMI Christian Music Publishing). Used by permission.

BLESS / BLESSED
1. Johnson Oatman Jr., Edwin O. Excell, "Count Your Blessings," 1987, public domain.
2. Don Moen, "Blessed Be the Name of the Lord," ©1986, Integrity's Hosanna! Music. All rights reserved. Used by permission.
3. Don Moen is a songwriter, worship leader, and recording artist. He is a multiple Dove Award nominee, and his work "God with Us" won a Dove Award. In addition to his writing and recording, Don makes time to tour domestically and abroad and has performed with artists such as Chris Tomlin, Twila Paris, Sara Groves, and Paul Baloche. For many years Don served as president of Integrity Music and executive vice-president/creative director for Integrity Media. Don is founder and chief creative officer of the Don Moen Company in Nashville, where he resides with his wife, Laura.
4. Written for this book by Don Moen. Used with permission.
5. Kirk Kirkland, Babbie Mason, "I Will Bless the Lord," ©2006, Praise and Worship Works (ASCAP) Singing Bush Music. Used by permission.

6. Kirk Kirkland is a songwriter, concert artist, worship leader, and studio singer. He has sung background vocals on the recordings of such artists as CeCe Winans, Steve Green, Alan Jackson, Phil Stacey, and the Gaither Vocal Band. He sings occasionally as a back-up singer at Nashville's Grand Ole Opry. As a songwriter, he has collaborated with Babbie Mason, Jamie Harvill, Mike Harland, Dennis and Nan Allen, and Kim Allen. Since 1999 Kirk has led Evidence Ministries (evidenceministries.org), a concert ministry that has brought him to stages nationally and around the world. Recently Kirk finished a master's degree in counseling and is using this training in ministry as the Minister of Pastoral Counseling at Judson Baptist Church in Nashville, where he is also the minister of music and worship (judsonbaptist.com). Kirk has been married to Julianne since March 1999. They welcomed a baby boy, Campbell, in May 2009. They currently reside in Nashville.
7. Written for this book by Kirk Kirkland. Used with permission.

BLOOD

1. Unknown origin, "O the Blood of Jesus," public domain.
2. Lewis E. Jones, "There Is Power in the Blood," 1899, public domain.
3. Elvina M. Hall, John T. Grape, "Jesus Paid It All," 1868, public domain.

BULWARK

1. Martin Luther, "A Mighty Fortress Is Our God," 1529, public domain.
2. William J. Reynold, *Companion to Bapist Hymnal,* © Broadman Press, 25.

CROSS

1. George Bennard, "The Old Rugged Cross," 1912, public domain.
2. Keith Getty, Stuart Townend, "The Power of the Cross," © 2005, ThankyouMusic (Admin. by EMI Christian Music Publishing). Used by permission.
3. Keith Getty, gettymusic.com. Used with permission.
4. William J. Gaither, Gloria Gaither, "The Old Rugged Cross Made the Difference," ©1970 William J. Gaither, Inc. ARR UBP of Gaither Copyright Management.

5. Gaither, Gloria. *Something Beautiful,* (New York: Faith Words, 2007), 262-64.

DAYS OF ELIJAH

1. Robin Mark, "Days of Elijah," © 1996 Daybreak Music, Ltd.

2. Robin Mark, "Days of Elijah," *Worship Leader,* Jan./Feb. 2007.

3. Robin Mark, <www.robinmark.com>.

DIADEM

1. Edward Perronet, John Rippon, Oliver Holden, "All Hail the Power of Jesus' Name," 1779, public domain.

2. Chris Machen, "Crown Him" © 1991 Desert North Music (Admin. by Word Music Group, Inc.) Word Music, LLC (a div. of Word Music Group, Inc.). All rights reserved. Used by permission.

3. Written for this book by Chris Machen. Used with permission.

EBENEZER

1. Robert Robinson, "Come, Thou Fount of Every Blessing," 1758, public domain.

EL SHADDAI / ALMIGHTY / MIGHTY

1. Wayne Watson, "Almighty" © 1990 Material Music (Admin. by Music Services). Used by permission.

2. Wayne Watson is a Dove Award-winning songwriter, solo artist, and Grammy Award nominee. He has had twenty-three number-one singles on Christian radio, including "Friend of a Wounded Heart," with Claire Cloninger; "Watercolour Ponies"; and "Another Time, Another Place." He gave a groundbreaking, emotionally charged performance of "Another Place, Another Time" with fellow artist Sandi Patty on NBC-TV's "The Tonight Show"—an event that was deemed a defining moment in Christian music's move to wider audiences. In the late 1990s his inspirational hit "For Such a Time as This" became a centerpiece theme of CBS-TV's then highly rated series *Touched by an Angel.* Wayne wrote this piece for this book. Used with permission

EXALT / EXTOL

1. Kirk and Deby Dearman, "Above All Else," © 1988 Integrity's Hosanna! Music.

2. Kirk and Deby are prolific songwriters. One of their best-known songs is "We Bring the Sacrifice of Praise." Their songs have been recorded by Integrity Music, Maranatha! Music, and Promise Keepers, and many are now found in contemporary hymnals. Their songs have also been recorded on several Messianic music projects. In addition to their songwriting, they are popular worship leaders.

Before settling in Franklin, Tennessee, the Dearmans toured and lived in Europe for seven years. They cofounded a performing arts troupe that toured cathedrals with worship music. They've led worship for the Christian Celebration of the Feast of Tabernacles in Jerusalem as well as numerous concerts in Germany, Holland, England, and Belgium. Kirk wrote this contribution for this book. Used with permission.

GLORY

1. Elisha A. Hoffman, John H. Stockton, "Down at the Cross," public domain.

2. William J. Gaither, Gloria Gaither, "All the Glory Belongs to Jesus," © 1988 William J. Gaither, Inc., ARR UBP of Gaither Copyright Management.

3. Unknown, "Gloria Patri," second century, public domain.

4. Babbie Mason, Donna Douglas, "In All of His Glory," © 1990 Word Music, LLC (a division of Word Music Group, Inc.), BMG Songs, Inc. (Admin. by BMG Music Publishing), Pamela Kay Music (Admin. by EMI Christian Music Publishing). Used by permission.

5. Babbie Mason is a well-known contemporary gospel singer. She was born and raised in Jackson, Michigan. She spent twenty years as a church pianist, choir director, and public school teacher before starting her own ministry in 1984. The following year, Babbie received top honors in the songwriting and vocal categories at the annual Christian Artists' Music Seminar. In 1990 she gained wide recognition with her Dove Award-nominated album "With All My Heart." The following year,

another of her albums contained several number-one singles and was also nominated for a Dove Award. This piece was written for this book by Babbie Mason and is used with permission.

GRACE

1. Julia H. Johnson, Daniel B. Towner, "Grace Greater than Our Sin," 1911, public domain.
2. John Newton, "Amazing Grace," 1779, public domain.

HOLY / HOLINESS

1. Geron Davis, "Holy Ground," © 1983, Meadowgreen Music Company/ Songchannel Music.
2. Nancy Gordon, Jamie Harvill, "Firm Foundation," © 1994 Integrity's Hosanna! Music, Integrity's Praise! Music.
3. Nancy Gordon has penned more than 300 songs and is a four-time Dove Award nominee. Her songs include "Firm Foundation," "Because We Believe," and "Come Expecting Jesus." Nancy created the character "Miss Patty Cake Praise" and was the creative consultant and primary writer on the NAPPA gold award-winning Itegrity Music "Just for Kids" Lullaby Tapes. She currently ministers with Through Mother's Heart Ministry. She lives in the Mobile, Alabama, area. Nancy wrote this piece for this book, and it is used with permission.
4. Claire Cloninger, David Clydesdale, "Holy Is He," © 1985, Word Music, LLC, Royal Tapestry Music (a division of Word Music Group, Inc.), Admin. by Brentwood-Benson Music Publishing, Inc.) Used by permission.
5. Claire Cloninger is a best-selling lyricist and author. She writes for church choirs as well as for artists. She has won six Dove Awards for her lyric writing, and her songs have been recorded by a variety of artists that include Don Moen, Sandy Patti, Amy Grant, Wayne Watson, and B. J. Thomas. Claire wrote a new second verse for "The Star-Spangled Banner" after being commissioned by the National Statue of Liberty Centennial Committee, which was used during the centennial celebration and at Disney World during the patriotic centennial

extravaganza. She has authored fourteen books. Her book "Dear Abba" was nominated in the devotional category for the ECPA Gold Medallion Award. She has recently co-authored a series with her sons, Curt and Andy, titled "E-mail from God." Claire lives with her husband, Robert, near Mobile, Alabama. This piece was written for this book and is used with permission.

6. Claire Cloninger, "Heartbeat of My Holiness," © 1996, Juniper Landing Music.

7. Giglio, Louie, *I Am Not but I Know I Am* (Sisters, Oreg.: Multnomah Books, 2005), 103. Used by permission.

HOLY SPIRIT

1. Dottie Rambo, David Huntsinger, "Holy Spirit, Thou Art Welcome," ©1977, John T. Benson Publishing Co. (ASCAP)/Bridge Building Music, Inc. (BMI) (Admin. by Brentwood-Benson Music Publishing, Inc.) All rights reserved. Used by permission.

2. David Huntsinger is a songwriter, arranger, producer, and studio musician. He has written with Dottie Rambo with whom he credited the classic children's musical "Down by the Creekbank" and the chorus "Holy Spirit, Thou Art Wecome." His producing credits include Andy Griffith, Carmen, and many custom recordings. David and his wife, Bonnie, live in Nashville. This piece was written for this book and is used with permission.

HOPE

1. Edward Mote, William Bradbury, "The Solid Rock," 1834, public domain.

HOSANNA

1. Brenton Brown, Paul Baloche, "Hosanna," ©2005, 2006, Integrity's Hosanna! Music Thankyou Music (Admin. by EMI Christian Music Publishing). Used by permission.

2. Brenton Brown, brentonbrown.com/blog. Used by permission.

IMMANUEL / EMMANUEL

    1. "O Come, O Come, Emmanuel," public domain.

INCARNATE WORD

    1. Charles Wesley, Felix Mendelssohn, "Hark! The Herald Angels Sing," 1739, public domain.

    2. Latin hymn ascribed to John Francis Wade, "O Come, All Ye Faithful," 1743, public domain.

    3. Words anonymous, Felice de Giardini, "Come, Thou Almighty King," 1764, public domain.

JEHOVAH / YAHWEH

    1. John Hughes, William Williams, "Guide Me, O Thou Great Jehovah," 1745, public domain.

JERUSALEM / NEW JERUSALEM

    1. Frederick E. Weatherly, Michael Maybrick, "The Holy City," 1892, public domain.

    2. Joseph Bromehead, "Jerusalem, My Happy Home," 1785, public domain.

JORDAN

    1. Samuel, American Folk Hymn, "On Jordan's Stormy Banks I Stand," 1787, public domain.

    2. John Hughes, William Williams, "Guide Me, O Thou Great Jehovah," 1745, public domain.

KINGDOM

    1. Timothy Dwight, Aaron Williams, "I Love Thy Kingdom, Lord," 1801, public domain.

    2. Isaac Watts, John Hatton, "Jesus Shall Reign Where'er the Sun," 1719, public domain.

    3. H. Ernest Nichol, "We've a Story to Tell to the Nations," 1896, public domain.

4. Ibid.

LAMB OF GOD

1. Dennis Jernigan, "You Are My All in All," ©1991, Shepherd's Heart Music, Inc. Used by permission.

2. Dennis Jernigan is a songwriter, worship leader, and recording artist. He has written some classic worship songs such as "We Will Worship the Lamb of Glory," "Thank You," "Great is the Lord Almighty," "Who Can Satisfy My Soul (There Is a Fountain)," "I Belong to Jesus," "Nobody Fills My Heart Like Jesus," and "You Are My All in All." Dennis and his wife, Melinda, live with their nine children on a farm in rural Oklahoma. Dennis wrote this piece for this book, and it is used by permission.

3. Greg Nelson, Phill McHugh, "Lamb of Glory," © 1982, Shepherd's Fold Music (a division of EMI Christian Music Publishing), River Oaks Music Company (a division of EMI Christian Music Publishing.)

4. Greg Nelson is a composer, arranger, orchestrator, and producer for numerous albums that include recordings of Sandi Patti, Larnelle Harris, Steve Green, Scott Wesley Brown, and other contemporary Christian artists. Many of his albums have gone gold, and he has received several Dove awards. He has written musical standards such as "People Need the Lord," "Jesus, Love to Me," and "Lamb of Glory." Greg and his wife, Pam, have two adult children and two grandchildren. They live in Brentwood, Tennessee. Greg wrote this piece for this book. It is used by permission.

LILY OF THE VALLEY

1. Charles W. Fry, William S. Hays, "I Have Found a Friend in Jesus, 1881, public domain.

MAGNIFY

1. Dick and Mel Tunney, "O Magnify the Lord," © 1982, Meadowgreen Music Company (Admin. by EMI Christian Music Publishing).

2. Written for this book by Melodie Tunney. Used by permission. Dick and Mel Tunney met in the late 1970s in the Christian group TRUTH. Dick later responded to a call from the award-winning group, The

Imperials, to travel as a keyboard player. Six months later the couple married and settled in Nashville. Mel became a studio singer, and along with fellow studio singers Bonnie Keen and Marty McCall began the group First Call. In 1986, Christian artist Sandi Patty hired Dick as musical director and pianist and First Call as her backup group. The "Let There Be Praise" tour covered 150 cities in 18 months and launched First Call on a concert ministry of its own while Dick remained on tour with Sandi Patty. The Tunneys have won 10 Dove Awards and one Grammy for their song "How Excellent Is Thy Name," recorded by Larnelle Harris. The Tunneys have two grown daughters and live in the Nashville area.

MAJESTY

1. Jack Hayford, "Majesty," © 1981 Rocksmith Music (Admin. by Brentwood-Benson Music Publishing, Inc., 741 Cool Springs Blvd., Franklin, TN 37067).
2. *Worship His Majesty,* by Jack Hayford, © 2000 Jack Hayford, published by Regal Books, Ventura, CA, 93003. Used by permission.

MORNING STAR

Charles W. Fry, William S. Hays, "I Have Found a Friend in Jesus," 1881, public domain.

NOEL

1. Traditional English Carol "The First Noel," thirteenth century, public domain.

OMNIPOTENT

1. John W. Peterson, "It Took a Miracle," © 1948, renewed 1976 by John W. Peterson Music Company. All rights reserved. Used by permission.

PEACE

1. Horatio G. Spafford, Philip P. Bliss, "It Is Well with My Soul," 1873, public domain.

RANSOM

1. Henry F. Lyte, Mark Andres, "Praise, My Soul, the King of Heaven," 1834, public domain.

REDEEM / REDEEMER

1. Eric Wyse, Dawn Rodgers Wyse, "Wonderful, Merciful Savior," © 1989 Word Music, LLC (a division of Word Music Group, Inc.) Dayspring Music, LLC (a division of Word Music Group, Inc.). Used by permission.

2. Dawn Rodgers is a gifted songwriter and graphic artist. She uses her artistic talents in both the mediums of art and music to the glory of God. Married to songwriter/producer Eric Wyse and mother of their two children, she makes her home in Franklin, Tennessee, where she owns and operates a graphic design company. Dawn often collaborates with other songwriters, but the beloved worship song "Wonderful, Merciful Savior" was co-written with her husband. Eric is Director of Music at St. Bartholomew's Church in Nashville. He studied piano, organ, and church music at Cedarville University in Ohio and is currently studying business and theology at Aquinas College. The contribution to this book was written by Dawn Rodgers Wyse and is used by permission.

REIGN / SOVEREIGN

1. Charles Wesley, John Darwall, "Rejoice, the Lord Is King," 1744, public domain.

REJOICE

1. Gary Sadler, Paul Baloche, "Rise Up and Praise Him," © 1996, Integrity's Hosanna! Music.

RIGHTEOUS / RIGHTEOUSNESS

1. Sandra Corbett, "I Worship You, Almighty God," © 1982, Integrity's Hosanna! Music.

ROCK

1. Edward Mote, William B. Bradbury, "The Solid Rock," 1834, public domain.

2. Augustus M. Toplady, Thomas Hastings, "Rock of Ages," 1776, public domain.

SABOATH (OR SABBAOTH)

1. Martin Luther, "A Mighty Fortress Is Our God," 1529, public domain.

SAVIOR

1. Carrie Breck, Grant Colfax Tullar, "Face to Face with Christ, My Savior," 1898, public domain.

2. Bob Farrell, Greg Nelson, Sandi Patti Helvering, "There Is a Savior," © 1986 Straightway Music Careers—BMG Music Publishing, Inc., Greg Nelson Music Lehsem Music, LLC, Sandi's Songs Music (a division of EMI Christian Music Publishing) (Admin. by BMG Music Publishing) (Admin. by EMI Christian Music Publishing) (Admin. by Gaither Copyright Management).

3. Bob Farrell holds a bachelor of arts degree in economics from the University of Houston. He has been a prolific composer for many years. He is co-creator of "HERO, The Rock Opera" with longtime friend Eddie DeGarmo. Bob has also written songs for many other artists including Eric Clapton, Wynonna Judd, Stacio Orrico, Amy Grant, Cliff Richards, Jaci Velasquez, Sandi Patty, Lonestar, and others. He has also cowritten several significant concept works over the past few years: "Le Voyage," "Savior," and "Emmanuel." His accomplishments include multiple Dove and Grammy nominations, winning six Dove awards. Bob has two daughters and four grandsons and lives in Nashville with Jayne, his wife of 38 years. Bob Farrell wrote this piece for this book, and it is used by permission.

TABERNACLE

1. Marc Byrd, Steve Hindalong, "God of Wonders," © 2000 New Spring, Storm Boy Music, Meaux Mercy (Admin. by Brentwood-Benson Music Publishing, Inc.) (Admin. by EMI Christian Music Publishing).

2. Words from Habakkuk 2:20, Music by George F. Root, "The Lord Is in His Holy Temple," public domain.

WORSHIP

1. Redman, Matt, *The Unquenchable Worshiper* (Ventura, Calif.: Regal Books, 2001), 102-103. Used by permission.
2. Matt Redman, "The Heart of Worship," © 1999, Thankyou Music (Admin. by EMI Christian Music Publishing). Used by permission.
3. Tomlin, Chris, *The Way I Was Made* (Sisters, Oreg.: Multnomah Publishers, 2005), 21-22. Used by permission.

ZION

1. Isaac Watts, Robert Lowry, "We're Marching to Zion," 1707, public domain.

RESOURCES USED

Arthur, Kay. *Lord, I Want To Know You.* Sisters, Oreg.:
    Multnomah Books, 1992.

Barclay, William. *New Testament Words.* Louisville, Ky.:
    Westminster Press, 1964.

Butler, T., ed. *Holman Bible Dictionary.* Nashville:
    Broadman and Holman, 1991.

Layman's Bible Book Commentary. Nashville:
    Broadman Press, 1983.

Osbeck, Kenneth W. *Amazing Grace: 366 Inspiring Hymn Stories for Daily
    Devotions.* [CITY & STATE]: [PUBLISHER, YEAR].

Peterson, William J., and Ardythe Peterson. *The Complete Book of Hymns:
    Inspiring Stories About 600 Hymns and Praise Songs.*
    [CITY & STATE]: [PUBLISHER, YEAR].

Unger's Bible Dictionary. Chicago: Moody Press, 1974.

Vine, W. E. *Vine's Expository Dictionary of Old and New Testament Words.*
    [CITY & STATE]: Revell, 1981.

Webster's Word Histories, [CITY]: Merriam-Webster Inc., Publishers, 1989.

ACKNOWLEDGMENTS

I offer my sincere thanks to the following people—songwriters and artists—who gave their insights into the words we sing:

Paul Baloche

Brenton Brown

Claire Cloninger

Kirk and Deby Dearman

Bob Farrell

Steve Fry

Gloria Gaither

Keith Getty

Louie Giglio

Nancy Gordon

Steve Green

Jack Hayford

David Huntsinger

Dennis Jernigan

Kirk Kirkland

Chris Machen

Robin Mark

Babbie Mason

Don Moen

Martha Munizzi

Greg Nelson

Matt Redman

Chance Scoggins

Chris Tomlin

Dick and Mel Tunney

Wayne Watson

Eric Wyse and Dawn Rodgers Wyse

"A true road map for worship pastors with great directions for every turn along the way."

—MARK HARRIS
4HIM

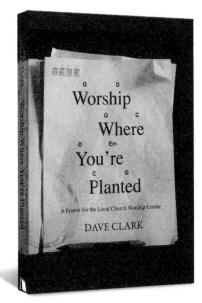

Worship Where You're Planted tackles issues such as transitioning between worship leaders, navigating traditional and contemporary music styles, and building rapport with the congregation. With wisdom and understanding, Dave Clark helps churches find the balance between who and what God called us to be and the constantly changing demands of worship ministry.

Worship Where You're Planted
A Primer for the Local Church Worship Leader
By Dave Clark
ISBN 978-0-8341-2555-1

www.BeaconHillBooks.com

Available wherever books are sold.